The Pope and the World

He for [two thousand] years
    has lived in the world;
he has seen all fortunes,
    he has encountered all adversaries,
he has shaped himself
    for all emergencies.

If ever there way a power on earth
    who had an eye for the times,
who has confined himself
    to the practicable,
and who has been happy
    in his anticipations,
whose words have been facts,
    and whose commands prophecies,
such is he
    in the history of the ages,
who sits from generation to generation
    in the chair of the Apostles,
as the Vicar of Christ
    and the doctor of His Church.

Cardinal John Henry Newman, *Idea of a University*

MINUTE MEDITATIONS
FROM THE POPES

Jesus makes Peter the first Pope: "Feed My lambs....Feed My sheep" (Jn 21:15-17).

MINUTE MEDITATIONS FROM THE POPES

MINUTE MEDITATIONS FOR EVERY DAY
TAKEN FROM THE WORDS OF POPES
FROM THE TWENTIETH CENTURY

Compiled and Edited
by
REV. JUDE WINKLER, O.F.M. Conv.

Illustrated

CATHOLIC BOOK PUBLISHING CORP.
New Jersey

CONTENTS

Dedicated to Fr. Bonaventure Jezierski, O.F.M. Conv., and Sr. Vincentia Jachemska, F.S.S.J., who through their simplicity and gentleness taught me to love the Church.

IMPRIMI POTEST: Mark Curesky, OFM Conv.
Minister Provincial of St. Anthony of Padua Province (USA)

NIHIL OBSTAT: Francis J. McAree, S.T.D.
Censor Librorum

IMPRIMATUR: ✠ Patrick J. Sheridan, D.D.
Vicar General, Archdiocese of New York

(T-175)

© 1994 Catholic Book Publishing Corp., N.J.

Printed in Hong Kong   ISBN 978-0-89942-175-9

INTRODUCTION

"Whoever hears you hears Me. Whoever rejects you rejects Me. And whoever rejects Me rejects the One Who sent Me" (Lk 10:16).

Since the beginning of the twentieth century, there has been an avalanche of material produced by the Holy Fathers for the instruction of the faithful. Yet much of this material is relatively unavailable to the everyday Catholic.

The most that many Americans tend to hear about the teaching of the Magisterium is what is featured on the religion page of the local newspaper, and the account given there is very often slanted with an anti-Catholic bias.

This book is intended to present some of that teaching in a form that makes it available to the busy Catholic. It gives an overview of the various topics covered by the Popes of this century. The format used is that of the "Minute Meditations Series," whose main purpose is to provide brief spiritual reading and reflection for each day.

To achieve this purpose it has been necessary at times to condense and adapt the quotations from the Popes. For example, sentences, clauses, or phrases have been deleted without indication and gaps have been bridged by supplying words. Despite these accidental changes, the text represents a faithful rendering of the thought of the Holy Pontiffs.

We express gratitude to the editor of the *Osservatore Romano,* for allowing us to use and adapt the English translation of the Holy Father's remarks.

In order to encourage minute meditation in the classical sense of the term, we have added a pertinent Scripture text for the theme of the day as well as a brief prayer.

The Scripture text serves as a reminder of the Church's commitment to the Word of God and her constant exhortation to the faithful to make profuse use of it. Readers can thus obtain a daily taste of that Word related to the theme of the day.

The prayer at the end of each reflection enables readers to apply the theme of the saintly Popes to their everyday lives in such a way as to aid them in their spiritual growth.

As you read and meditate upon these texts, we ask you to allow yourself to be consoled, edified, challenged, and called to conversion. May the Holy Spirit lead you to greater fidelity to the call of Christ, especially as expressed through the teaching of our Shepherds.

HERE is an appointed time for everything, and a time for every activity.

—Eccl 3:1

REFLECTION. Time is a gift from God; it is a question posed by God's love to our free and fateful answer. We must be sparing of time in order to use it well in the intense activity of our life of work, love, and suffering.

Idleness or boredom has no place in the life of a Christian. —*Pope Paul VI*

PRAYER. *O Lord, help me to live each moment of my days as if it were the first, last, and only moment that I have to live. Let me make the most of every instant of time.*

FFER your bodies as living sacrifices, holy and spiritual to God— which is your spiritual worship.

—Rom 12:1

REFLECTION. Christian life is a sacrifice. Sacrifice inspired by charity has the merit of bringing us into conformity with the earthly life of Jesus.

For He became our brother and died for us in order to assure us of joy and glory forever.

—*Pope John XXIII*

PRAYER. *O Lord, teach me the profound meaning of sharing in the Cross of Jesus, Your Son, so that I may live forever in Your love.*

I WILL hear what the Lord God will speak. For He will speak peace to His people and His holy ones. —Ps 85:8

JAN.
3

REFLECTION. Modern society is barely conscious of the ills that assail it. It conceals its miseries beneath a prosperous, glittering, and trouble-free exterior.

In such a society the Immaculate Virgin manifests herself to an innocent child of Lourdes. —Pope Pius XII

PRAYER. *Make me always attentive to Your Word, O Lord. And let me be humble and simple enough to embrace it with openness and joy.*

 LOVE is patient, love is kind. It does not envy, does not boast, and is not self-seeking. —1 Cor 13:4

JAN.
4

REFLECTION. Loving is not easy. It presupposes affective maturity, willpower, the capacity for self-control, and an attitude of self-denial and giving.

It is necessary to learn how to love. This is an apprenticeship that requires years of commitment. —Pope John Paul II

PRAYER. *Lord, You called St. Elizabeth Ann Seton to share her life in charitable service to Your people. Teach me at the same school of love and help me to follow her example of generosity.*

MAKE disciples of all nations ..., teaching them to obey all that I have commanded you. —Mt 28: 19-20

JAN. 5

REFLECTION. Today, faced with the contradictions of the adult world and the rapidity of change, evangelizers could become discouraged and be tempted to limit their missionary effort.

We must revive the Master's invitation to the whole world! To all creatures! To the ends of the earth! —*Pope John Paul II*

PRAYER. *O Lord, grant me the courage that inspired St. John Neumann to leave his homeland in order to serve the American people. Teach me how to invite others to share the Faith.*

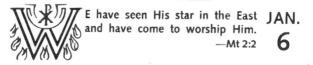

WE have seen His star in the East and have come to worship Him. —Mt 2:2

JAN. 6

REFLECTION. Once a star led the Magi to set out on their journey to the Lord. And it may be that the star has not yet appeared in the sky that you see.

Nonetheless, in your soul there is that same interior light that guided the Magi.

—*Pope John Paul II*

PRAYER. *The Magi followed their star to present their gifts of gold, frankincense, and myrrh to the Child Jesus. Teach me to bring Him the gifts of my heart, hope, and love.*

9

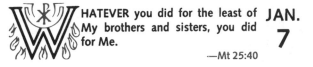

WHATEVER you did for the least of My brothers and sisters, you did for Me.

JAN. 7

—Mt 25:40

REFLECTION. Jesus identified Himself with the poor and the defenseless. Thus, what we do for them is done for Him, and the service we fail to render them is service denied to Him.

Gross disparities of wealth between nations, classes, and persons reenact the parable of the rich man and Lazarus. *—Pope John Paul II*

PRAYER. *O Lord, you condemned the rich man for his neglect of Lazarus his poor brother. Never let me forget to share with my poor sisters and brothers.*

LORD, teach us to pray, just as John taught his disciples.

JAN. 8

—Lk 11:1

REFLECTION. Prayer is the breath of the Mystical Body, its conversation with God, the expression of its love and its striving toward the Father. *—Pope Paul VI*

PRAYER. *Lord Jesus, as You taught Your disciples to pray, so now teach Your Church to pray. Send Your Spirit into my heart so that I may join my voice to Yours as I give glory to the Father.*

10

NE of the soldiers pierced Jesus' side with a spear, and at once blood and water flowed out.

—Jn 19:34

REFLECTION. The Heart of Christ overflows with divine and human love and is abundantly rich with the treasures of all the graces that our Redeemer acquired by His Life, Passion, and Death.

It is truly the unfailing fountain of the love that His Spirit pours forth into all the members of His Mystical Body. —*Pope Pius XII*

PRAYER. *Lord Jesus, You are my love, You are my life. Guide, protect, forgive and embrace me.*

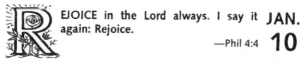

EJOICE in the Lord always. I say it again: Rejoice.

—Phil 4:4

REFLECTION. Be happy, rejoice in Christ's love, and live from His strength. True, you cannot always be healthy or successful.

However, you can always be with Christ and find strength at His side.

—*Pope John Paul II*

PRAYER. *O Lord, give me perspective during the trials of my life and humility during my successes. Fill me with Your Spirit of joy both in good times and in bad, for You are my only true joy.*

EHOLD, I am with you always, until the end of the world.

JAN. 11

—Mt 28:20

REFLECTION. You may say that it is hard to think of yourself as a brother or sister of Someone Who died so long ago. But no, Jesus is alive today and always!

This is our Faith. This is the source of everything it means to be a Christian.

—*Pope John Paul II*

PRAYER. *When the road becomes long and weary, O Lord, and I begin to doubt Your presence in my life, show me once again that You are always with me.*

 HOSE who wish to be My disciples must deny themselves, take up their cross daily and follow Me.

JAN. 12

—Lk 9:23

REFLECTION. Every Cross that we see in the world becomes a silent reminder for us.

The true victory that overcomes hatred in the world is ultimately self-sacrifice, in constant fidelity flowing from the power of love.

—*Pope John Paul II*

PRAYER. *Your Cross, Lord Jesus, is a sign of life and an invitation to sacrifice. When I am confronted with selfishness and hate, give me the courage to embrace the Mystery of the Cross. Help me to remember that only love truly conquers.*

EAVING the Sanhedrin, the Apostles rejoiced that they had been found worthy to suffer disgrace for the sake of the Name. —Acts 5:41

REFLECTION. Let us strive to be true Catholics, convinced Catholics, unwavering Catholics, good Catholics. Ours cannot be a watered down, approximate, and camouflaged Catholicism.

Above all, it cannot be a Catholicism that implies denying by our behavior what will bring us and our Separated Brethren mutually closer. —Pope Paul VI

PRAYER. Lord, let me never be ashamed of who I am; neither let me deny my beliefs.

F you love those who love you, what reward will you get?
—Mt 5:46

REFLECTION. We may be tempted to show respect only for the great ones of the earth and to reserve our love for our own family and friends.

But Christ teaches us that, for good or ill, what we do to the least of our brothers and sisters we do to Him. —Pope John Paul II

PRAYER. Make my love large, O Lord, so that it extends beyond my family and friends to those who most need my concern. Let me reach out to them in concrete ways.

YOU are in the spirit, if only the Spirit of God dwells in you.

—Rom 8:9

JAN. 15

REFLECTION.   The Spirit of God is the Spirit of life, Who is capable of causing life to burst forth even where everything seemed dead and withered.

That is why we can and must have confidence. Not only can we, but we must!

—*Pope John Paul II*

PRAYER. *Come, Spirit of Life, inflame my heart with the light of faith and the fire of love.*

IF you forgive others when they sin against you, your heavenly Father will also forgive you.

—Mt 6:14

JAN. 16

REFLECTION.   If peace is to reign in your hearts, you must be willing to forgive, to forgive completely and sincerely.

No community can survive without forgiveness. No family can live in harmony, no friendship can endure, without repeated forgiveness.   —*Pope John Paul II*

PRAYER. *O Lord, it can be so difficult to forgive. Make me dwell upon how much You have forgiven me, so that I may remember how much I should be willing to forgive others.*

LL who want to be My disciples must deny themselves.

—Mk 8:34

REFLECTION. Attaining happiness requires a rigorous personal ascetism whose function is to bring order into the human person.

It is a tragic lie to teach people that happiness can or even should be reached by abandoning oneself to the inclinations of instinct, without any self-denial. —*Pope John Paul II*

PRAYER. *O Lord, St. Anthony the Abbot traveled out into the desert in order to learn the ways of self-denial. May I too find the desert in my life and learn from You.*

IRST of all, I ask that supplications, prayers, petitions, and thanksgivings be offered for everyone. **JAN. 18**

—1 Tim 2:1

REFLECTION. I ask you to pray for those who cannot pray and also for those who do not know how to pray.

Pray too for all who have lost faith in God and in His mercy.

—*Pope John Paul II*

PRAYER. *Lord, help me to commit myself to an apostolate of prayer. Let me pray for those whom I love, but especially for those who desperately need my love.*

PREACH the Word; be prepared in season and out of season.

—2 Tim 4:2

JAN.
19

REFLECTION. We strongly deny the assertion that there is no obligation for us to put the message of Christ at the disposal of all.

Indeed, we claim with full conviction that it is our right and our duty to do no less.

—*Pope John Paul II*

PRAYER. *O Lord, you have given me such a precious gift by letting me hear and accept Your Word. Grant me the courage to proclaim it to others. Make me a missionary in my neighborhood, at my work, and with my family.*

WATCH and pray that you may not enter into temptation.

—Mt 26:41

JAN.
20

REFLECTION. There exists a close connection between holiness of life and the promotion of a more human way of life in society, for it is from a converted and reconciled heart that goodness and justice flow in human relations.

Time and energy given to the life of the spirit is not time and energy taken away from service. —*Pope John Paul II*

PRAYER. *Call me back to the fountain of your grace, O Lord. Refresh my spirit and give me spiritual energy to share with others.*

FOR the foolishness of God is wiser than human wisdom, and the weakness of God is stronger than human strength.

JAN.
21

—1 Cor 1:25

REFLECTION. Despite her youth, St. Agnes experienced the victorious strength of the love of Christ. Sustained by that inner force, she was able to "conquer overwhelmingly."

May she be your model of courage and generosity in every event of your life.

—*Pope John Paul II*

PRAYER. *Teach me to trust in Your strength, O Lord, especially when I feel overwhelmed by my weakness. Help me to recall that I can conquer only by surrendering to Your love.*

NO servants are greater than their master. If they have persecuted Me, they will persecute you also.

JAN.
22

—Jn 15:20

REFLECTION. You must understand that faithful service to Christ and His Church will not always earn you the world's praise.

On the contrary, you will sometimes receive the same treatment as the Lord: rejection, contempt, and even persecution.

—*Pope John Paul II*

PRAYER. *O Lord, when I suffer the price of being Christian, especially at work, at school, or even in my family, remind me that You will never abandon those who suffer in Your Name.*

COME to Me, all you who suffer and are burdened, and I will refresh you.

—Mt 11:28

REFLECTION. Sorrow is an isolated thing in the natural world. For Jesus, however, it is part of an encounter.

Thus, those of you who are sick, who are unfortunate, who are dying may lack all things, but not Jesus on the Cross. He is with you. He is indeed with you. —*Pope John Paul II*

PRAYER. *O Lord, when I experience the pain of life, hold my hand and embrace me with Your love. Let me always know that Your Cross is a promise that You will never abandon me.*

YOU will have trouble in this world. But take heart! I have overcome the world.

—Jn 16:33

REFLECTION. If you nourish your life with personal and liturgical prayer, if you are supported by the advice of a spiritual guide, you will not be afraid to face the world.

On the contrary, you will face it with a calm, positive, and open mind. —*Pope John Paul II*

PRAYER. *O Lord, St. Francis de Sales spoke about how people can encounter You in the ordinary circumstances of their life. May his life and teachings call me to a greater commitment to spiritual growth.*

AY all of them be one, Father, just as You are in Me and I am in You.

—Jn 17:21

REFLECTION. Paul's conversion reminds us that a sincere change of heart is essential for the spiritual progress of individual Christians as well as for full unity among them.

Only by a change of attitude and behavior toward one another can Christ's disciples remove the obstacles to such unity. —*Pope John Paul II*

PRAYER. *At the Last Supper, O Lord, You prayed that Your flock might always be one. Teach me to surrender my prejudices and selfishness so that I may always be one with all Your children in Your love.*

 EACH [the Faith] to your children and to your children's children.

—Dt 4:9

REFLECTION. Marriage is a communion of life. It is the home. It is work. It is concern for the children.

It is also joy and leisure in common.

—*Pope John Paul II*

PRAYER. *O Lord, Sts. Timothy and Titus taught the early Churches about the sanctity of family life. May they intercede for the members of my family to make them holy and filled with Your peace.*

DO not be afraid. I bring you good tidings of great joy.

—Lk 2:10

REFLECTION. As people, we are meant to have human joys: the joy of living, the joy of love and friendship, the joy of work well done.

As Christians, we have cause for further joy: like Jesus, we know that we are loved by God our Father. —*Pope John Paul II*

PRAYER. *O Lord, the Angels announced the birth of Your Son, which brought great joy to the world. May I experience that joy in my heart and share that joy with those who have lost hope.*

LISTEN to my instruction and be wise; do not ignore it.

—Prov 8:33

REFLECTION. The way to the heart very often passes through the mind.

Today, throughout the length and breadth of the Church there is need for a new effort of evangelization and catechesis directed to the mind. —*Pope John Paul II*

PRAYER. *God of wisdom, instruct me in Your ways. Help me dedicate myself to learning more about the Faith, so that like St. Thomas Aquinas my mind and heart may be united in Your love.*

THE Kingdom of heaven is like leaven that a woman took and mixed with three measures of flour until the whole dough was leavened. —Mt 13:33

JAN.
29

REFLECTION. It must be borne in mind that to proceed gradually is the law of life in all its expressions.

Therefore, in human institutions, too, it is not possible to renovate for the better except by working from within them, gradually.

—*Pope John XXIII*

PRAYER. *O Lord, help me to build Your Kingdom upon this earth. Fortify me with Your courage, teach me Your prudence, and grant me Your vision of a world built upon love.*

———————

EVEN though you have ten thousand tutors in Christ, you do not have many fathers, for I became your father through Christ Jesus in the Gospel. —1 Cor 4:15

JAN.
30

REFLECTION. Christ desires to be newly present to this contemporary world with all the explosive force of His Mystery of love.

He wishes to meet the people of today through teachers who are true educators, drawn by Christ. —*Pope John Paul II*

PRAYER. *I promise to be Your voice, O Lord, in a world that needs to hear Your message. I promise to conform my life to that message so that what I proclaim in words may be seen in my actions.*

21

YOU have become followers of the Churches of God that are in Judea in Christ Jesus.

—1 Thes 2:14

REFLECTION. The Church is the unifying effect of the love of Christ for us. She can herself be considered a living sign, a Sacrament of unity and of love.

To love is her mission.

—*Pope Paul VI*

PRAYER. *Thank You, O Lord, for the Church, Your gift of love to the whole world. Teach me to be a faithful child of that Church, willing to live and die in order to give witness to that love.*

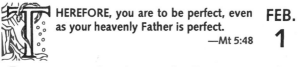

THEREFORE, you are to be perfect, even as your heavenly Father is perfect.

FEB.
1

—Mt 5:48

REFLECTION. "To be perfect" means to love God not a little, but a great deal.

It means not to stop at the point at which we have arrived, but with His help to progress in love.

—*Pope John Paul I*

PRAYER. *Purify my intentions, O Lord, so that my love may be pure. Give courage to my heart, so that my love may be ever more perfect.*

WHEN the eight days of her purification were fulfilled, they took Him up to Jerusalem to present Him to the Lord. —Lk 2:22

FEB.

2

REFLECTION. The origin, nature, destiny, and history of humanity are bound up in that Infant by the very fact of His birth among us.

Without the knowledge of that history our human nature would remain an inpenetrable enigma. —*Pope Pius XII*

PRAYER. *Lord Jesus, Simeon and Anna greeted You when You were brought into the Temple as an infant by Mary Your Mother and Joseph Your foster father. May I be as anxious to recognize Your Presence in our midst.*

BETTER off poor, healthy, and fit than wealthy and afflicted in body. More precious than gold is health and well-being. —Sir 30:14-15

FEB.

3

REFLECTION. Grace builds upon nature. The Gospel does not make inhuman demands on us.

It enlightens, elevates, and perfects what is human through the power of God's grace. —*Pope John Paul II*

PRAYER. *In Your Incarnation, Lord Jesus, You taught us that our humanity is not to be despised, but rather to be esteemed as a gift of Your love. Make me aware that what I eat, how I exercise, and other ways I care for my body are forms of appreciation for that gift.*

23

VEN so let your light shine before others so that they may see your good works and give glory to your Father in heaven.

—Mt 5:16

REFLECTION. Allow the light and the healing presence of Christ to shine brightly through your lives.

In that way, all those who come in contact with you will discover the loving kindness of God.

—*Pope John Paul II*

PRAYER. *Make my heart transparent, O God, so the light of Your love shines through me. May that light shatter the darkness of a world filled with fear and selfishness.*

 LESSED are they who suffer persecution for justice' sake, for theirs is the Kingdom of heaven.

—Mt 5:10

REFLECTION. Love gives suffering meaning and makes it acceptable. It is possible to have love without suffering; but suffering without love has no meaning.

Suffering accepted with love, as Christ and the Saints accepted it, acquires an inestimable value. —*Pope John Paul II*

PRAYER. *O Lord, teach me the lessons of love that guided St. Agatha as she suffered and died for her Faith. Give me the courage to see my own suffering as an encounter with Your Cross.*

BLESSED are you when people reproach you, and persecute you, and speaking falsely, say all manner of evil against you for My sake. —Mt 5:11

**FEB.
6**

REFLECTION.   Suffering for the sake of love, truth, and justice is a sign of fidelity to the God of life and of hope.

It is the blessedness of those who suffer for Christ, who fall to the ground like grains of wheat and are promised life and resurrection.

—*Pope John Paul II*

PRAYER. *Lord Jesus, You proclaimed blessed those who suffer for the sake of justice. Let me never stand by the wayside when my brothers and sisters are suffering unjustly.*

REJOICE insofar as you are partakers of the sufferings of Christ, that you may also rejoice with exultation in the revelation of His glory. —1 Pt 4:13

**FEB.
7**

REFLECTION.   Jesus is the joy of the earth; He is the physician of every human infirmity. He is personified in every person who suffers, arousing compassion and generous love.

Jesus, therefore, is present always and everywhere.   —*Pope Paul VI*

PRAYER. *Come, Lord Jesus. Help me to recognize Your Presence in my life, especially in my pain. Help me to know that You have joined Your sufferings to mine, so that I may join my suffering to Yours.*

UT whoever causes one of these little ones who believe in Me to sin, it would be better for that person ... to be drowned in the depths of the sea. —Mt 18:6

FEB. 8

REFLECTION. Children learn to do what they see others doing.

For this reason, they should learn from you how to be strong, industrious, temperate, happy, and devout, upright citizens and exemplary Christians. —*Pope John Paul II*

PRAYER. *You taught that we should not give scandal to the little ones, dear Lord. Help me to conform my life to Your will so that whatever I say or do may be filled with Your truth.*

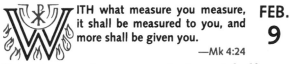

ITH what measure you measure, it shall be measured to you, and more shall be given you.

—Mk 4:24

FEB. 9

REFLECTION. Love cannot stop at half measures, as you well know.

Love must be ready to offer itself as far as the very ultimate in generosity.

—*Pope John Paul II*

PRAYER. *You taught, Lord Jesus, that the measure with which we measure will be measured back to us. Let the measure of my love be generous. May I never hold back when the cost is great.*

I AM the vine, and you are the branches. Those who abide in Me and I in them bear much fruit, because apart from Me you can do nothing. —Jn 15:5

FEB. 10

REFLECTION. In a single word, be Saints! Holiness is the most powerful force that leads human hearts to Christ. Remember that verse of the Gospel about the vine and the branches.

In the union of the branches with the one vine is the concrete source and the sure measure of one's apostolic activity. —*Pope John Paul II*

PRAYER. *You are the vine, O Lord, and we are the branches. Keep me united to You and nourish me with Your love so that I may bear abundant fruit.*

T HUS in the chosen city He has given me rest.... I have struck root among the glorious people, in the portion of the Lord, His heritage. —Sir 24:11-12

FEB. 11

REFLECTION. Lourdes is a prophecy of justice and peace, where there is no room for pride and hardness of heart.

Indeed, Lourdes is where this hardness is dissolved by one's witness of charity, mercy, serene resistance to evil, human solidarity, and sincere and moving generosity. —*Pope John Paul II*

PRAYER. *O Mary, you appeared to the humble young woman, St. Bernadette Soubirous, to call us to conversion. Help me to respond to that call with generosity.*

FOR me to live is Christ and to die is gain. But if to live in the flesh is my lot, this means for me fruitful labor.

FEB.
12

—Phil 1:21-22

REFLECTION. Welcome Christ into your lives. Without the experience of this interior meeting with Christ, life can all too easily be wasted on illusory and consumerist experiences.

These obviously include the suicidal experience of drugs or the egoistic one of using our neighbor and rejecting solidarity.

—*Pope John Paul II*

PRAYER. *Clarify my vision, O Lord, so that I may see clearly Your truth and choose it with all my heart, my strength, and my love.*

I BEG you, be imitators of me, as I am of Christ.

FEB.
13

—1 Cor 4:16

REFLECTION. Nobody is a Christian for oneself alone.

The gift of faith is given to us so that by word and example we may become witnesses before others.

—*Pope John Paul II*

PRAYER. *Shower Your grace upon me, O Lord. May my faith be a fruitful tree that feeds the hunger of many. May it be a fountain to quench the thirst of those whose faith is weak.*

EAL the sick. . . . Freely you have received; freely give.

—Mt 10:8

REFLECTION. The person who has been evangelized goes on to evangelize others.

It is unthinkable that people should accept the Word and give themselves to the Kingdom without becoming persons who bear witness to it and proclaim it in turn.

—Pope Paul VI

PRAYER. O Lord, Sts. Cyril and Methodius spent their lives to share the Word of God. Teach me to share that Word, especially with those who are living without hope.

ING praise to the Lord with the harp, with the harp and melodious song. With trumpets and the sound of horns sing joyfully.

—Ps 98:5-6

REFLECTION. As a manifestation of the human spirit, music performs a function that is noble, unique, and irreplaceable.

When music is truly beautiful and inspired, it speaks to us more than all the other acts of goodness, virtue, and peace.

—Pope John Paul II

PRAYER. When I hear beautiful music, O Lord, it lifts up my spirit. May I always cherish things of beauty, music, art, nature, and anything else that can draw me closer to You.

ALL the promises of God find their "Yes" in Christ; and therefore through Him also rises the "Amen" to God to our glory.　　—2 Cor 1:20

REFLECTION.　In Christ we find hope, because He is the symbol of hope, friendship, unending love, and the Father's indescribable affection for every individual.

We know that all the promises and hopes find their complete fulfillment in Christ, because in Christ God's very word has found its "Yes."　　　　　　　　　　*—Pope John Paul II*

PRAYER. *Lord Jesus, be the source and the goal of my life. Be my all, and lead me to the Father.*

SO now, O children, give heed to me and do not reject instruction and wisdom.
　　　　　　　　　　—Prov 8:32-33

REFLECTION.　Mary is the clearest and surest sign that God always comes to us with His love. She sings with all her being that whatever we receive from God is grace.

The Virgin is our true teacher in the journey of faith.　　　　　　　　　　*—Pope John Paul II*

PRAYER. *O Lord, the seven founders of the Servites followed the example of Mary Your Mother in serving God's People. Help me to learn that same generosity and live it everyday of my life.*

Y Father, if this cup cannot pass away unless I drink it, Your will be done.

FEB.
18

—Mt 26:42

REFLECTION. There is a higher wisdom: a wisdom that reveals the true meaning of our human weakness and our pain. That wisdom is revealed in Christ.

He knows what it is to suffer; He experienced it on the road to Calvary. —*Pope John Paul II*

PRAYER. *O Lord, the wisdom of the world tells me to think only of myself. Teach me to enter into the mystery of surrendering to the Father's will. Let me say, "Not my will, but Your will be done."*

 HOROUGHLY wash me from my guilt, and cleanse me of my sin. For I acknowledge my offense.

FEB.
19

—Ps 51:4-5

REFLECTION. Only those persons who recognize that they are sinners, in need of salvation because they cannot save themselves, only they can extend their hands to Jesus as to their Savior.

—*Pope John Paul; II*

PRAYER. *O Lord, help me to admit that I need others in my life, that I cannot make it alone. And of all of those whom I need, I need You most, for You are my God and my all.*

OD created humankind in His image; in the image of God He created them. Male and female He created them. —Gn 1:27

FEB.
20

REFLECTION. In a world that often reduces sex to the pursuit of pleasure, and in some cases to domination, the Church has a special mission.

She is to place sex in the context of conjugal love and of generous and responsible openness to parenthood.

—*Pope John Paul II*

PRAYER. *O Lord, let me always treat my sexuality as a holy and precious gift. Let me never use it to manipulate others or even myself.*

HIS is My Body, which is being given for you. Do this in remembrance of Me. —Lk 22:19

FEB.
21

REFLECTION. Christ's love for us: behold the Eucharist! Love that gives itself, love that remains, love that communicates itself, love that multiplies itself, love that sacrifices itself.

The Eucharist is the love that unites us and the love that saves us.

—*Pope Paul VI*

PRAYER. *O Holy Banquet, in which Christ is received, the memory of His Passion is recalled, the soul is filled with grace, and a pledge of future glory is given to us!*

BE shepherds of Christ's flock that is under your care ..., not lording it over those entrusted to you but being examples to [them]. —1 Pt 5:2-3

REFLECTION. Authority is a duty, a burden, a debt, a ministry to others, to lead them to the life of God. It is a channel, an obligatory, necessary, but saving channel, and it is called the care of souls.

This is the pastoral function. —*Pope Paul VI*

PRAYER. *O Lord, protect and guide those who have been given authority in the Church, especially Pope N. and our Bishop N. Make them generous and courageous in the exercise of their ministry.*

IF anyone does not love the Lord Jesus Christ, let that person be anathema. Come, O Lord.
—1 Cor 16:22

REFLECTION. It is He, it is only He Who can quench the deep and mysterious thirst of your spirits.

Jesus, Jesus; He is the light and salvation of the world and of each of us.

—*Pope Paul VI*

PRAYER. *St. Polycarp was so in love with You, Lord Jesus, that nothing else was important to him, not even his life, for he died a Martyr. Grant me that same single-mindedness and that same courage.*

T once the father of the boy exclaimed, "I do believe; help what little faith I have."

FEB.
24

—Mk 9:24

REFLECTION. We must be convinced of the necessity of having a living, authentic, and active faith. That is all the more true today, when we face so many difficulties.

It is not enough to have a vague, weak, or uncertain faith.

—*Pope John XXIII*

PRAYER. *O Lord, I often feel like the man in the Gospels who asked You to help what little faith he had. Fill my heart with Your gift of faith, and let my faith be active and living.*

Y child, conduct your affairs with meekness, and you will be loved by those whom God accepts.

FEB.
25

—Sir 3:17

REFLECTION. The meek endure conflict and jealousy, rivalries that arise within families and among neighbors. They do not, however, passively accept situations of injustice.

They are anything but indifferent, but they do not respond to violence with violence, to hatred with hatred.

—*Pope John Paul II*

PRAYER. *O Lord, let me always fight injustice when I see it, but by being willing to die for justice, never to kill for it.*

IVE in a manner worthy of the Lord and please Him in all ways, bearing fruit in every good work.

—Col 1:10

REFLECTION. In a secularized world, to speak and act in the name of Jesus can bring opposition and even ridicule. It often means being out of step with the majority opinion.

Yet if we look at the New Testament, we find encouragement for perseverance in this testing of our faith. —*Pope John Paul II*

PRAYER. *Lord Jesus, help me never to measure my morality by the standards of an unbelieving world. Let the Gospel be the source of my beliefs and the goal of my actions.*

HE fear of the Lord is the beginning of knowledge, but fools despise wisdom and discipline.

—Prov. 1:7

REFLECTION. Science can purify religion from error and superstition. Religion can purify science from idolatry and false absolutes.

Each can draw the other into a wider world, a world in which both can flourish.

—*Pope John Paul II*

PRAYER. *O Lord, the world tells us that our faith and our science are opposed. It tells us we must live either by our mind or by our heart. Teach me Your truth where mind and heart, science and faith are no longer opposed.*

E careful not to forget the Lord, your God, by neglecting His commandments, laws, and decrees.

FEB.
28

—Dt 8:11

REFLECTION. The temptation today is to try to build a world for oneself, forgetting the Creator and His design and loving Providence.

But sooner or later we must come to grips with this: that to forget God, to feign the death of God, is to promote the death of humankind and of all civilization. —*Pope John Paul II*

PRAYER. *O Lord, You are the source of all that lives and the goal of all of creation. May I learn of Your love from creation, and may I respect creation because of Your love.*

ARY said, "Behold the handmaid of the Lord. May it be done to me according to your word."

FEB.
29

—Lk 1:38

REFLECTION. Mary, you are the Mother of the Church and the Model of every vocation.

Help us respond by saying "Yes" to the Lord when He calls us to collaborate in the Divine Plan of salvation.

—*Pope John Paul II*

PRAYER. *Mary, our Mother, let me imitate your eager response to the message of the Angel. Teach me to say "Yes" to the Lord's call to make His love incarnate in this world.*

GOD saw that all He had made was very good. And there was evening, and there was morning—the sixth day. —Gn 1:31

REFLECTION. The new generations need to be helped to grow as free persons, to love truth and to be faithful to it. The search for the true, the beautiful, and the good is not a pragmatic exercise, but rather a cultural and ethical one.

It is a service to human development and a way for evangelization. —*Pope John Paul II*

PRAYER. *That which is beautiful in the world speaks of You, O Lord. Let me encourage art, music, literature, whatever is good and true so that these may be seen as celebrations of Your love.* _____

IF you hold to My teaching, you are really My disciples. Then you will know the truth, and the truth will make you free. —Jn 8:31-32

REFLECTION. Being a Christian is not a secondary, questionable, changeable thing; it is not a subjective ideology.

It is truth that happily transfigures and vivifies. The truth will make you free.

—*Pope Paul VI*

PRAYER. *Lord Jesus, when I act as a Christian, I am most true to myself. But when I deny who I am by sinning, I am denying the very core of who I am: Your child. Let me always live in the truth of the children of God.*

PERSONS who say, "I love God" but hate their brothers or sisters are liars. For how can they who do not love those whom they see love God Whom they do not see!
—1 Jn 4:20

MAR.
3

REFLECTION. In today's world, torn by indifference, division, hatred, and oppression, fraternal communion founded on love is an eloquent example of universal reconciliation in Christ. —*Pope John Paul II*

PRAYER. *O Lord, teach me to lay aside the petty differences and annoyances that can shade my relationships with others. Let me treat them with as much respect as I would treat You.*

THE harvest indeed is great, but the laborers are few. Pray therefore the Lord of the harvest to send forth laborers into His harvest. —Mt 9:37-38

MAR.
4

REFLECTION. Let us not only take care to defend ourselves from the contagion of evil but also to promote the good, sustain it, give witness to it, defend it, and multiply it.

We must take responsibility for the fact that the world is suffering from evil stemming from our lukewarmness.

—*Pope John XXIII*

PRAYER. *Send me, O Lord, into the field for the harvest. Send me, to give witness to Your Word and Your love.*

WHOEVER hears you hears Me. Whoever rejects you rejects Me. And whoever rejects Me rejects the One Who sent Me. —Lk 10:16

MAR. 5

REFLECTION. The Church cannot say what is bad is good, nor can she call valid what is invalid.

She cannot fail to proclaim Christ's teaching, even when this teaching is difficult to accept.

—*Pope John Paul II*

PRAYER. *O Lord, give me the courage to accept and live the teaching of the Church. May I always be willing to review my life and hear the Church's call to conversion.*

GOD said, "I give you every seed-bearing plant on the face of the earth and every tree that has fruit with seed on it." —Gn 1:29

MAR. 6

REFLECTION. We cannot say we love the land and then take steps to destroy it for use by future generations.

I urge you to be sensitive to the many issues affecting the environment and to unite to seek the best solutions to these pressing problems.

—*Pope John Paul II*

PRAYER. *Enkindle my heart, O Lord, to love the created world, and awaken my mind to discern how to preserve and celebrate this gift with which you have entrusted us.*

WE know that all things work together unto good for those who
love God, who have been called according to His purpose. —Rom 8:28

REFLECTION. Remember well, a Christian, especially a Catholic, must be strong. I mean
spiritual and moral strength. A follower of
Christ should not be afraid.

Christians should feel surrounded by an atmosphere of Providence that makes all things
work out. —*Pope John XXIII*

PRAYER. *Teach me to trust in Your Providence, O Lord, for it is so easy to be filled
with fear and to despair. Guide me through
the dark valleys of my life until I come home
to Your Kingdom.*

BLESSED are they whose fault is taken
away, whose sins are covered. Blessed
are they to whom the Lord imputes no
guilt. —Ps 32:2

REFLECTION. Even the memory of our sins
does not discourage us any longer.

We realize that God's mercy is greater than
our sins and that God's pardon is a proof of
His faithful love for us.

—*Pope John Paul II*

PRAYER. *I give You thanks, O Lord, for Your
wondrous mercy. May I never allow the guilt
of my sins to separate me from the love and
forgiveness that You offer.*

IN the [Gospel] the justice of God is revealed, from faith to faith, as it is written: "The just person lives by faith."

MAR. 9

—Rom 1:17

REFLECTION. May the sacred flame of the Faith burn on the domestic hearth, and may parents forge and fashion the lives of their children in accordance with this Faith.

Then youth will be ever ready to acknowledge the royal prerogatives of the Redeemer and to oppose those who wish to exclude Him from society. —*Pope Pius XII*

PRAYER. *Enkindle that flame of faith in my family, Lord Jesus, so that we may give witness to God's love in a powerful way. Grant us the wisdom to discern Your will and the courage to fulfill it.*

FOR in Christ Jesus neither circumcision nor uncircumcision has any value. The only thing that counts is faith that works through love.

MAR. 10

—Gal 5:6

REFLECTION. People today more willingly listen to witnesses than to teachers.

If they do listen to teachers, it is because these teachers are also witnesses.

—*Pope Paul VI*

PRAYER. *O Lord, may I always give witness to my Faith through my actions as well as my words. May my actions always be a proclamation of Your love.*

ESUS was led into the desert by the Spirit to be tempted by the devil ... spending forty days and forty nights [there]. **MAR. 11**

—Mt 4:1-2

REFLECTION. The season of Lent keeps inviting us, in a pressing way, to meditate on this great truth: love is of God.

This is a living, present reality that we should never forget. —*Pope John Paul II*

PRAYER. *Lord Jesus, as You spent forty days in the desert to prepare for Your mission, grant that my Lenten preparation may prepare me to celebrate the Holy Mysteries of Your Death and Resurrection.*

 E have gifts differing according to the grace that has been given us ... to be used according to the proportion of faith. —Rom 12:6 **MAR. 12**

REFLECTION. If the members who constitute the parish are numerically many, so are the gifts that the Holy Spirit incessantly distributes.

So also are the initiatives that He awakens there according to the grace given to each member. —*Pope John Paul II*

PRAYER. *O Lord, the gifts that You entrust into our care are intended for the good of all. Help me to examine my conscience as to whether I have sufficiently shared my talents with others, and enable me to be ever more generous in my use of Your gifts to me.*

EEK first the Kingdom of God and His justice, and all these things [such as clothes and food] will be given you.

MAR.
13

—Mt 6:33

REFLECTION. This is the time to act, to do. A Church that chooses to remain inactive could not possibly be a faithful Church. It would not be a living Church.

It could neither confront nor overcome the difficulties that we face in our days.

—*Pope John XXIII*

PRAYER. *Never allow me to sit back, O Lord, when I see injustice or hurt. Keep me fully engaged in the struggle to further the Kingdom of God.*

 O not say, "I am too young." To whomever I send you, you shall go. Whatever I command you, you shall speak.

MAR.
14

—Jer 1:7

REFLECTION. In the face of the phenomenon of the diminished number of those consecrated to the priesthood and the religious life, we cannot remain passive, not doing as much as we possibly can.

Above all, we can pray very much.

—*Pope John Paul II*

PRAYER. *Send workers into Your vineyard, O Lord. Give priests, religious, and laity a sense of responsibility to preach Your call to conversion to a world in need of Your message.*

AY the God of hope fill you with all joy and peace in believing, that you may abound in hope.

—Rom 15:13

REFLECTION. We cannot live without hope. We have to have some purpose in our life, some meaning to our existence. We have to aspire to something.

Without hope, we begin to die. Hope comes from God, from our belief in God.

—*Pope John Paul II*

PRAYER. *I need You, O Lord. I cannot live without You. Be present to me, now, and every moment of my life to imbue me with hope that never dies.*

OVE consists in this: not that we have loved God, but that He has first loved us, and sent His Son as expiation for our sins.

—1 Jn 4:10

REFLECTION. God's love for us is freely given and unearned, surpassing all we could ever hope for or imagine.

His love for us does not depend on whether we have merited or are worthy of it.

—*Pope John Paul II*

PRAYER. *Thank You, O Lord, for a love that knows no measure, and is so wondrous that I cannot even begin to fathom its greatness. I am overwhelmed at Your love for me. I love You, Lord Jesus.*

CAME to you in weakness and fear and **MAR.** much trembling ... with a demonstration of the Spirit's power.

17

—1 Cor 2:3

REFLECTION. Our human brothers and sisters need to meet others radiant with serenity, joy, hope, and charity, in spite of the hardships and contradictions that overtake them.

To be a witness to God's power operating in human frailty is not to alienate humanity, but to propose to it ways to freedom.   —*Pope Paul VI*

PRAYER. *Fill me with Your love, O Lord, so that I may freely choose to love. Teach me to share that love, especially with people who seem all but unlovable.*

———

HRIST has set us free. Therefore, stand **MAR.** fast and do not submit again to the yoke of slavery [to sin].

18

—Gal 5:1

REFLECTION. If we are to respect people in their integrity, we must educate them to do good with a sense of responsibility; with a capacity for self-discipline and also with the external help of law and authority.

—*Pope Paul VI*

PRAYER. *O Lord, by my words and actions may I teach others the importance of living a morally ordered life. May I show others that this type of life is not enslavement but the true freedom of the children of God.*

O Joseph, arising from sleep, did as the Angel of the Lord had commanded him, and took unto him his wife.

MAR.
19

—Mt 1:24

REFLECTION. Joseph obeyed. Filled with joy, he offered up the tremendous human sacrifice that was asked of him. He would be the father of the one born not of flesh, but from love.

He was publicly the husband, but really only the guardian, the witness and defender of the immaculate virginity and the Divine Maternity of Mary. —*Pope John XXIII*

PRAYER. *Joseph, spouse of the Virgin Mother of God, teach me increasingly all the Divine truth and all the human dignity contained in the vocation of spouses and parents.*

———————

 HEN the sun rises, they withdraw and couch in their dens. People go out to their work until the evening.

MAR.
20

—Ps 104:22-23

REFLECTION. The spirituality of work consists in the awareness that through our work, we can place ourselves in a relation with our ultimate destiny.

We can become an ally of the living God.

—*Pope John Paul II*

PRAYER. *O Lord, when my work becomes heavy and boring, remind me that You have called me to be a co-creator of this world. Together, we shall build the Kingdom of God.*

THE world with its desires is passing away, but the person who does the will of God abides forever.

—1 Jn 2:17

MAR.
21

REFLECTION. The world is often closed in its riches or its power, corroded by conflicts, and drunk with violence or sexual release.

It is faith that bestows a liberation and puts the individual's faculties in order.

—*Pope Paul VI*

PRAYER. *Protect me, O Lord, when I am tempted by the lies of the world. Let me never use people, either others or myself, as objects. May I always treat them and You with sacred respect.*

KEEP me, O God, for in You I trust.... My Lord are You. Apart from You I have no good.

—Ps 16:1

MAR.
22

REFLECTION. We are working for the Kingdom of God, and we do not do so with the gloomy spirit of those who see only insufficiences or perils.

We work with the firm trust of those who know that they can count on the victory of Christ.

—*Pope John Paul II*

PRAYER. *Direct my eyes, O Lord, upon the truth of the Kingdom, upon the love that conquers, and upon the hope that never fails.*

ACH of you must give according as you have decided in your heart, not grudgingly or under compulsion. For God loves a cheerful giver. —2 Cor 9:7

REFLECTION. Because all are entrusted with the vast area of charity and material assistance, I invite you to give generously.

Give for the maintenance and support of seminarians, for the formation of the laity, in particular of catechists, for the construction of churches, schools, hospitals, and social work. —*Pope John Paul II*

PRAYER. *O Lord, grant that I may remember that what I have received from Your Providence, I have received in trust. Teach me to use these gifts with great generosity.*

VER this [salvation] you greatly rejoice, though now for a little while you are sorrowful by various trials. —1 Pt 1:6

REFLECTION. The Spirit creates joy, and joy is effusive.

This, too, is a testimony that you can and must offer to people of our time, so often made cold and unhappy by selfishness.

—*Pope Paul VI*

PRAYER. *O Lord, fill my heart with joy both so that I may experience true Gospel joy and so that I may share that joy with those who have forgotten the true meaning of joy.*

AND the Word was made flesh and dwelt among us. And we saw His glory ... as the only-begotten of the Father. —Jn 1:14

MAR.
25

REFLECTION. The Divine is united to the human. The invisible has become visible. The infinite has assumed a human form.

Humanity has been accepted into the unity of the Divine Person of the Word.

—*Pope John Paul II*

PRAYER. *Lord Jesus, as Your dear Mother Mary gave her "fiat" when she responded, "Let it be done to me according to Your word" (Luke 1:38), so too may I learn to cooperate with God's will.*

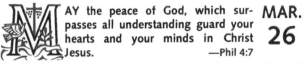

MAY the peace of God, which surpasses all understanding guard your hearts and your minds in Christ Jesus. —Phil 4:7

MAR.
26

REFLECTION. Do not seek to be numbered among the learned and clever whose numbers seem destined by the combination of circumstances to increase. Be truly poor, meek, eager for holiness, merciful, pure of heart.

Be among those who bring to the world the peace of God. —*Pope Paul VI*

PRAYER. *Teach me Your ways, Lord Jesus, for You were meek as a lamb in Your suffering, and yet You transformed the world. Teach me the true wisdom of Your Kingdom.*

IF I have all faith so as to move mountains yet do not have charity, I am nothing. **MAR. 27**
—1 Cor 13:2

REFLECTION. Faith must be accompanied by charity, charity that unites us all with one another and with Christ.

It must be accompanied by charity that, under the inspiration and motion of the Divine Spirit, welds the members of the Mystical Body together by an unbreakable bond.

—*Pope Pius XII*

PRAYER. *O Lord, help me never to forget that I am my brother's and my sister's keeper. May I also learn to be vulnerable, so that I can accept their love and care of me.*

THE Law ... is speaking to those under the Law in order that ... the whole world may be made subject to God. **MAR. 28**
—Rom 3:19

REFLECTION. Christians do not estrange themselves from life in society. They assume its history and express its culture.

At the same time they strive to radiate to those around them the spiritual realities of which they are bearers. —*Pope John Paul II*

PRAYER. *Teach me the balance, O Lord, between celebrating that which is good in our world and being critical enough to discern that which is dangerous and selfish.*

DO not labor for the food that perishes, but for that which endures unto life everlasting, which the Son of Man will give you. —Jn 6:27

MAR.
29

REFLECTION. The Eucharist is in no way alien to the building of a new world. Rather, it is the principle and source of inspiration.

For the Lord Jesus is the foundation of a new humanity that is reconciled and fraternal.

—*Pope John Paul II*

PRAYER. *May the Sacrament of Your Body and Blood, O Lord, teach me to be bread that is broken to feed the hunger of a starving world and wine that is outpoured to satisfy the thirst of a world dying of spiritual thirst.*

WHATEVER you do in word or in work, do all in the Name of the Lord Jesus, giving thanks to God the Father through Him. —Col 3:7

MAR.
30

REFLECTION. Above all it is my conviction that all work is a fundamental dimension of human existence on the earth.

This is true of all work—from the simplest to the most difficult, from the less paying to the most rewarding. —*Pope John Paul II*

PRAYER. *Lord Jesus, let my work be productive and meaningful, and my attitude toward work be positive and generous. May I always remember that in my work I am working with You to recreate the world in Your image.*

LAVISHLY the just give to the poor. Their generosity shall endure forever; their horn is exalted in honor.

—Ps 112:9

REFLECTION. It is not enough for us to reach out and help those in need.

We must help them to discover the values that enable them to build a new life and to take their rightful place in society with dignity and justice. —*Pope John Paul II*

PRAYER. *O Lord, may I not be satisfied with handing the poor a fish when I can teach them how to fish. Let me not only fill their stomachs with food but also take the time and energy to fill their spirits with dignity.*

———————

WE pray always for you, that our God ... may by His power fulfill every good purpose of yours and every act prompted by your faith.—2 Thes 1:11

REFLECTION. Pray for the many spiritual and material needs of your families, your communities, the whole Church, and all of humanity.

Indeed, prayer is the first and greatest work of charity that we must do for our brothers and sisters.

—*Pope John Paul II*

PRAYER. *Lord Jesus, like the Apostles of old, I too come before You and ask You to teach me to pray. Let prayer be the light of my mind, the joy of my heart, and the life of my soul.*

MARTHA, you are anxious and troubled about many things. Yet only one thing is necessary. Mary has chosen the better part. —Lk 10:41-42

REFLECTION. Christian renunciation is an authentic way of Christian life. It implies a hierarchical classification of its goods and it stimulates us to choose the better part.

It gives us practice in self-control, and it establishes a mysterious economy of expiation, which makes us participants in Christ's redemption. —*Pope Paul VI*

PRAYER. *O Lord, let me remember that saying "Yes" to Your love also involves saying "No" to those things that separate me from that love.*

HAVING been justified therefore by faith, let us have peace with God through our Lord, Jesus Christ. —Rom 15:1

REFLECTION. Peace is not weakness, nor being indifferent.

It is the daughter of justice.

—*Pope John XXIII*

PRAYER. *Help me always to work for justice, O Lord, so that we may all experience peace. Let this be true especially in my own family, my own neighborhood, my own parish, and my own country. At the same time, remind me to pray for justice and peace in the whole world.*

THIS cup is the New Covenant in My Blood. Do this, as often as you drink it, in remembrance of Me.

APR.

4

—1 Cor 11:25

REFLECTION. We must strive to ensure that the celebration of the Divine Mysteries be given such a central place in the organization of pastoral activity that all apostolic activity will have its beginning and fulfillment therein.

For the Liturgy is the "summit and fount" of the Church's life and mission. —*Pope John Paul II*

PRAYER. *At the Last Supper, O Lord, You commanded Your disciples to "do this in remembrance of Me." May I fulfill this command by actively participating in the Liturgy.*

IF you have faith like a mustard seed, you will say to this mountain, "Move from here"; and it will move.

APR.

5

—Mt 17:19

REFLECTION. The Christian Faith does not destroy culture but purifies and uplifts it. It takes away nothing of genuine value from a society or nation.

The Christian Faith strengthens whatever is good for the betterment of all. —*Pope John Paul II*

PRAYER. *O Lord, You asked Christians to infuse Your values and Your teachings within the world. May the literature I read, the movies and the TV I watch, and the music I listen to, all give witness to my Faith.*

EHOLD how good and how pleasant it is where brothers and sisters dwell together as one.

—Ps 133:1

REFLECTION. Watch! Do not let the precious values of faithful married love and family life be taken away from you.

Do not reject them, or think that there is some other human prospect for happiness and human fulfillment.

—*Pope John Paul II*

PRAYER. *Shower Your love upon my family, O Lord. Let all of us be filled with concern for each other. Make us willing to sacrifice, ready to forgive, and generous with time and talent.*

ATHER, blessed are they who hear the Word of God and keep it.

—Lk 11:28

REFLECTION. When the Word of God is duly accepted and properly observed, it assures unity in families as well as stability in society.

It also assures an indestructible joy that will last beyond time and be transformed for all eternity into a life that suffers no decline.

—*Pope John XXIII*

PRAYER. *O Lord, in this time of chaos, I seek an ordered life for myself and my family. Let me find the source of that order in Your Word that gives life.*

ALL who believed were together and ... would sell their possessions and goods and distribute them among all according as anyone had need. —Acts 2:44-45

APR. 8

REFLECTION. Christians must share in the task of building up the city, creating new modes of neighborliness and relationship.

They must also perceive an original application of social justice and undertake responsibility for this collective future.

—*Pope Paul VI*

PRAYER. *O Lord, let me remember that every Christian is called to transform this world, to make it more just, more peaceful, and more loving. Help me to do my part.*

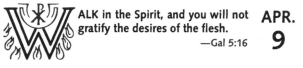

WALK in the Spirit, and you will not gratify the desires of the flesh. —Gal 5:16

APR. 9

REFLECTION. We must insist on the priority of ethics over technology, on the primacy of the person over things, on the superiority of the spirit over nature.

Humanity will be served if science and culture ally themselves with conscience.

—*Pope John Paul II*

PRAYER. *O Lord, the world proclaims that what is new must be good. Help me to remember that the dignity of the individual is of primary value, and it should never be compromised for convenience' sake.*

LET my prayer rise like incense before You; the lifting of my hands, like the evening sacrifice.

APR. 10

—Ps 140:2

REFLECTION. Pray also for your brothers and sisters and for all the children of the world, especially those who are poor and hungry.

Pray for those who do not know Jesus, for those who are alone and sad.

—Pope John Paul II

PRAYER. *O Lord, let my prayers for those in need rise up to Your heavenly throne like incense. Join the love found in these prayers with Your love and pour it down upon the parched hearts of this world.*

YES, when you seek Me with all your heart, you will find Me with you, says the Lord, and I will change your lot.

APR. 11

—Jer 29:13-14

REFLECTION. What is of greatest importance is that people be fired with loving enthusiasm for prayer.

In addition, they must spread the warmth of that flame to others with zeal and self-sacrifice.

—Pope John XXIII

PRAYER. *O Lord, may I learn from St. Scholastica, the sister of St. Benedict, the joy of speaking to and about God. May time spent in prayer not be seen as an obligation, but rather as the most meaningful part of my day.*

JESUS came and stood in the midst [of the disciples] and said to them, "Peace be with you!"

—Jn 20:19

REFLECTION. The peace of Christ is different from that of the world.

The peace of Christ surely does not remove trials and tribulations, but it is always a source of serenity and happiness. For it brings with it the fullness of life. —*Pope John Paul II*

PRAYER. *Lord Jesus, Your first words to Your disciples who were filled with guilt and confusion were "Peace be with you." Let me experience that peace in my life, a peace so profound that the trials and difficulties of life cannot disturb it.*

———

 FOR I am not ashamed of the Gospel; it is the power of God for the salvation of all who believe.

—Rom 1:16

REFLECTION. Those who deem themselves to be Christian must know this fact.

They are bound by conscience to the basic, imperative duty of bearing witness to the truth in which they believe and to the grace that has transformed their soul.

—*Pope John XXIII*

PRAYER. *O Lord, teach me to make my life ever more transparent and consistent, so that I may live ever more fully in Your truth.*

MAY your father and your mother have joy. May she who bore you be glad.
—Prov 23:25

APR.
14

REFLECTION. Responsible parenthood involves not only bringing children into the world, but also taking part personally and responsibly in their upbringing and education.

True love in the family is forever!

—Pope John Paul II

PRAYER. O Lord, let me value my family above my work, my career, and any other thing that might tempt me away from those whom I love.

I HAVE planted and Apollos has watered. But it is God Who has given the increase.
—1 Cor 3.6

APR.
15

REFLECTION. May prayers give wings to work, purify intentions, and be a defense against the longings of materialism.

And may work in its turn lead to the refreshing encounter with God in which humanity rediscovers its primordial vocation and the true meaning of its existence.

—Pope John Paul II

PRAYER. O Lord, teach me the balance between work and prayer. Help me to do my part in giving birth to the Kingdom of God, but let me also turn over to You that which only You can do.

59

EEK the Kingdom of God, and all these things will be given you as well.

—Lk 12:31

APR. 16

REFLECTION. The Church reaffirms the religious and supernatural values of penitence.

She invites everyone to accompany the inner conversion of the spirit with the voluntary exercise of external acts of penitence.

—Pope Paul VI

PRAYER. *O Lord, give me the courage and the wisdom to seek You above all other goods. Help me to see things with the proper perspective, so that food or leisure or work may never become the center of my life.*

ORGETTING what is behind, I strain forward to what is before, I press on toward the goal.

—Phil 3:14

APR. 17

REFLECTION. As Christians we should offer our memories to the Lord.

Thinking about the past will not alter the reality of your sufferings or disappointments, but it can change the way you look at them.

—Pope John Paul II

PRAYER. *Lord Jesus, I offer up to You my memories. Thank You for those wonderful days and events when I experienced Your love so clearly. Please heal those memories that still seem so far from Your love.*

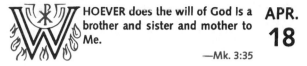

WHOEVER does the will of God is a brother and sister and mother to Me.

APR. 18

—Mk. 3:35

REFLECTION. The Christian family is a sacred institution. If it totters, if the norms that the Divine Redeemer laid down for it are rejected or ignored, then the very foundations of the state tremble.

Civil society stands betrayed and in peril. Everyone suffers. —*Pope John XXIII*

PRAYER. *O Lord, I often complain about all the dangers and difficulties in our society. Let me address these problems in a healthy way by recommiting myself to my own family.*

THE time is fulfilled, and the Kingdom of God is at hand. Repent and believe in the Gospel.

APR. 19

—Mk 1:15

REFLECTION. A sincere and zealous reformer will avoid extremes and never overstep the bounds of true reform.

The true reformer will always be united in the closest bonds with the Church and Christ, her Head. —*Pope Pius X*

PRAYER. *O Lord, we have heard that virtue lies in the middle, and that extremes bring division. Teach me to balance my opinions so that I may serve love and not my own pet theories.*

THE work of each will be manifested, for the Day of the Lord will disclose it. It will be revealed with fire.

—1 Cor 3:13

REFLECTION. How essential it is for the life of society that people not lose faith in their own work.

How essential it is that they not suffer disillusionment because of this work.

—*Pope John Paul II*

PRAYER. *Lord Jesus, help me to see my work as a calling from You. Enable me to regard my coworkers as people whom You have sent into my life for a reason.*

ANYWHERE two or three are gathered together in My Name, there am I in the midst of them.

**APR.
21**

—Mt 18:20

REFLECTION. In prayer the Church concentrates on Christ; she possesses Him, savors His Friendship, and is therefore in a position to communicate Him.

But by exercising faith, hope, and charity in prayer, she reinforces her power to communicate Christ. —*Pope John Paul II*

PRAYER. *O Lord, it can be so difficult to find time to pray. Give me the courage to set aside other things that keep me from prayer, and grant me the love to want to spend more time with You.*

BLESSED are the pure in heart, for they will see God.

—Mt 5:8

APR. 22

REFLECTION. All the pure in heart are, in a certain sense, mystics, because, as Christ proclaimed, they are candidates to "see God."

But we should all be pure in heart, all good, simple, and childlike. We should all be able to want, be able to yearn, be able to receive.

—*Pope Paul VI*

PRAYER. *Lord Jesus, this world so often teaches us to become complicated and cynical. Enable me to enjoy the simple things that are so easy to take for granted.*

WHAT I tell you in darkness, speak it in the light. And what you hear whispered, proclaim it from the housetops. —Mt 10:27

APR. 23

REFLECTION. Christians of these last years of the Second Millennium, you have an honorable yet burdensome task.

You must be bearers of the Word to those who have lost its full meaning and importance. —*Pope John Paul II*

PRAYER. *Make me a missionary of Your Word, O Lord. Let me not be ashamed of being a Catholic, but rather enable me to see my faith as something so precious that I want to share it with everyone whom I meet.*

RIDE on triumphant in the cause of truth and for the sake of justice; and may your right hand show you wondrous deeds. —Ps 45:4-5

APR.
24

REFLECTION. Let no one in your land be at ease while there is anyone whose human and Christian dignity is not respected and loved.

This is true whether that person is a man, a woman, a child, an elderly or sick person, or any child of God! —*Pope John Paul II*

PRAYER. *You taught us, Jesus, that whatever we do to the least of Your brothers and sisters we do to You. May I see and judge all persons as You do, and may I treat them with the same respect with which I would treat You.*

THROUGH my mouth the Gentiles should hear the Word of the Gospel and believe. —Acts 15:7

APR.
25

REFLECTION. The dynamism of new life is at work throughout history in apostolic service and in the mandate to pass on the Gospel.

In order to touch everyone's heart it must be translated into understandable and easily accessible language. —*Pope John Paul II*

PRAYER. *Lord Jesus, when St. Mark wrote his Gospel, he spoke of You in simple terms, presenting us with a Jesus Who truly shared in our humanity. Help me to have a simple faith, so that I may encounter You Who are both God and Man.*

YOU shall be witnesses for Me ... even to the very ends of the earth.

APR. 26

—Acts 1:8

REFLECTION. Every believer ought to be an active member of the Church.

Every Catholic lay person is invested with the right and has the duty to work in order to testify to and spread the Kingdom of God.

—Pope Paul VI

PRAYER. *O Lord, guide me so that I may know the work to which You call me to build up Your Church on earth. Let me respond to Your call with complete readiness and much generosity.*

DEEP waters cannot quench love, nor floods sweep it away.

APR. 27

—Song 8:7

REFLECTION. Do not be afraid of the demands of the love of Christ. On the contrary, be afraid of being fainthearted, of taking things lightly, of seeking your comfort, of being selfish.

Be afraid of everything that seeks to silence the voice of Christ Who addresses each person.

—Pope John Paul II

PRAYER. *Embolden my heart, O Lord, to love as You have loved. Let me not count the cost but rather trust that You will always make up what is lacking in me.*

REJOICE with those who rejoice. Weep with those who weep. Be of one mind toward one another.

APR. 28

—Rom 12:15-16

REFLECTION. Here is a model image of what the sentiments of the evangelizer should be:

A person who suffers with those who suffer, rejoices with those who rejoice, and gives self to all so that others may share an immense joy. —*Pope John Paul II*

PRAYER. *O Lord, grant that in my dealings with others, I may never succumb to rigidity. Help me to be willing to "walk in their shoes," so that I may respond to their needs and share in their lives.*

———

FOR I determined not to know anything among you, except Jesus Christ and Him crucified.

APR. 29

—1 Cor 2:2

REFLECTION. With Catherine of Siena and so many other "Saints of the Cross" let us hold on tightly to our most sweet and merciful Redeemer, Whom Catherine called Christ-Love.

In His pierced Heart is our hope.

—*Pope John Paul II*

PRAYER. *Teach me the logic of Your Cross, O Lord. Help me to understand the astounding love that You expressed through this act, and enable me to respond to that love with all my heart, soul, and strength.*

OU have not chosen Me, but I have chosen you and have appointed you that you should bear fruit.

APR.
30

—1 Cor 15:16

REFLECTION. Our Church is the Sacrament of God's love. She is a communion of faith and life. She is a mother and teacher.

She is at the service of the whole human family as it goes forth toward its ultimate destiny. —*Pope John Paul II*

PRAYER. *O Lord, You have given us the Church to help us transform our human society into the family of God. May I realize that the Church is my family, and thus always treat it with due love and respect.*

OW did this Man come by this wisdom and these miracles? Is He not the carpenter's Son?

MAY
1

—Mt 13:55

REFLECTION. Work is not something that people do for the sole purpose of earning a living; it is a human dimension that can and must be sanctified.

In this way, work will enable people to fulfill their vocation as creatures made in the image and likeness of God. —*Pope John Paul II*

PRAYER. *O Lord, grant that St. Joseph, patron of human work, will assist me in my work, in that vocation I have on earth. May he teach me to resolve the difficult problems connected with work.*

BECAUSE you are lukewarm, and neither cold nor hot, I am about to spit you out of my mouth.

**MAY
2**

— Rev. 3:15

REFLECTION. People in our modern society are threatened by the disease of superficiality, by complacency.

We must work in order to reacquire depth, that depth which is really the essence of the human person. —*Pope John Paul II*

PRAYER. *Lord Jesus, may I never be satisfied with easy answers to complex problems. May I always continue to pursue growth as a person, so that I may be most fully that which You intended me to be.*

JESUS said to the disciple, "Behold your Mother." And from that hour the disciple took her into his home.

**MAY
3**

—Jn 15:27

REFLECTION. Today my thoughts turn to Czestochowa where the Feast of the Black Madonna is being celebrated.

Many pilgrims are there, many of whom have come there on foot as a sign of devotion and penance.

—*Pope John Paul II*

PRAYER. *Dear Lord, may our Lady of Czestochowa make my Gospel witness ever more faithful. May she be my hope and the cause of my joy, leading me to You.*

O branch can bear fruit by itself.... So neither can you unless you abide in Me. **MAY 4**

—Jn 15:4

REFLECTION. The Heart of Christ still beats. It unites millions of other hearts.

The Church sees the beauty of these hearts, which will surely proclaim a spiritual acceleration in our modern world. —*Pope Paul VI*

PRAYER. *Let me see in Your Sacred Heart, O Jesus, a model of what I am called to be. Join my love to Yours, so that our love may build a new world.*

GUIDE me in Your truth and teach me, for You are God my Savior. **MAY 5**

—Ps 25:5

REFLECTION. We believe we are free because we liberate ourselves from what we have learned, because we get away from obedience and rules, because we entrust ourselves to the new and unknown.

But we often fail to notice that we are becoming followers of others' ideas and imitators of fashion imposed by others. —*Pope Paul VI*

PRAYER. *O Lord, grant me discernment to judge what is a passing fashion and what is eternal truth. May I be steadfast in my defense of that truth, even when that is an unpopular stance to take.*

N the contrary, whoever wishes to become great among you shall be your servant.

MAY 6

—Mt 20:26

REFLECTION. It is love that led Christ to serve, to give His life as a ransom for many. The word "to serve" no longer means an insupportable degradation of the human being's dignity.

In the sense Christ gave it, service acquires the highest moral value—dominion of self, heroism, sacrifice, boundless love. —*Pope Paul VI*

PRAYER. *Teach me, O Lord, that the measure of success in my life is how much I have loved. Let me love more each day of my life, until I finally come home to You, Who are pure love.*

OOSE the chains of injustice and untie the bonds of the yoke, set the oppressed free and break every yoke.

MAY 7

—Is 58:6

REFLECTION. Be careful to defend always and everywhere the just rights and true freedom of persons—without discrimination.

Such discrimination occurs when we become sensitive only to those victims whose ideas or convictions we share. —*Pope Paul VI*

PRAYER. *O Lord, teach me to reach out to all Your little ones, especially to those who have no one to defend them. Let me begin this service especially with those with whom I live, work, and pray.*

YET it was our infirmities that He bore, our sufferings that He endured.

—Is 53:4

REFLECTION. The Good News is this: that God loves us. He became human to share in our life and to share His life with us.

He walks with us every step of the way, taking our concerns as His own, for He cares about us. —*Pope Paul VI*

PRAYER. *O Lord, when I think of the things You have done and do for me, I am overwhelmed with gratitude. You are so good, so loving. Let my every breath, my every heartbeat remind me to thank You once again.*

WHO shall separate us from the love of Christ? Shall tribulation or distress or hunger or nakedness or danger or the sword? —Rom 8:35

REFLECTION. We must not be afraid of finding ourselves one day in a minority if we are faithful. We must not be embarrassed by unpopularity if we are consistent.

We must not care about being defeated if we are witnesses to truth and to the freedom of the children of God. —*Pope Paul VI*

PRAYER. *Lord Jesus, let me never run away and hide when courage is needed. Make me willing to fight for justice, even if that struggle leads me to the Cross.*

HE watches over household matters and eats not her food in idleness. Her children rise up and call her blessed.

MAY 10

—Prov 31:27-28

REFLECTION. The rearing and education of children should be the joint task of the father and mother, and there is certainly progress to be made in order that men should take their part in this task to a greater degree.

But it is only too clear that the role of the woman remains an essential one. —*Pope Paul VI*

PRAYER. *O Lord, now when the roles of parents are so often in confusion, help me to give of myself. Let me never do the minimum necessary, but rather always do the maximum.*

———————

 THE Lord, am your God. And you shall make and keep yourselves holy, because I am holy.

MAY 11

—Lv 11:44

REFLECTION. All are called to holiness, and it is possible to all. It is an invitation from the heart of God the Father Who sanctifies and divinizes us through the grace merited by Christ.

This grace is sustained by His Spirit, nourished by the Sacraments, and transmitted by the Church.

—*Pope Paul VI*

PRAYER. *Lord God, I do not consider myself to be holy, and yet You call me to holiness. Teach me Your ways and guide me so that I may respond to the call to be holy as You are holy.*

THIS is indeed a grace, if you endure the pain of unjust suffering because you are conscious of God.

—1 Pt 2:19

REFLECTION. Suffering is a necessary ingredient of holiness. Love is like it.

The love that Christ teaches us and that He first lived to give us an example is a merciful love, a love that atones and saves through suffering. —*Pope John Paul II*

PRAYER. *Lord Jesus, so often when people are in pain, they feel as if they are abandoned or are being punished. Help me to see Your love in those moments of doubt and join my suffering to Your own.*

DO not be frightened. But set apart Christ as Lord in your hearts.

—1 Pt 3:14-15

REFLECTION. Jesus is the center of history and of all things.

He is the One Who knows us and loves us, the Companion and Friend of our life, a Man of sorrow and of hope.

—*Pope Paul VI*

PRAYER. *Be the center of my life, Lord Jesus. Be closer to me than my own heart. Let our love be one, and our life be one, now and forever.*

UPON this rock I will build My Church, and the gates of hell shall not prevail against it.

MAY
14

—Mt 16:18

REFLECTION. Today the Church is alive. Despite all contrary appearances, the Church is united.

The Church is and remains the yeast in the dough, the signal among nations.

—Pope Paul VI

PRAYER. *Guide Your Church, O Lord, through these difficult times. Bestow upon her good and holy leadership. Send her committed members. Endow her with the courage to lead us home to You.*

AS the Father has loved Me, I also have loved you. Abide in My love.... Keep My commandments.

MAY
15

—Jn 15:9

REFLECTION. In the special manifestation to St. Margaret Mary, Christ pointed to His Heart as the symbol by which we are drawn to recognize and to acknowledge His love.

At the same time, He constituted it as a sign and pledge of His mercy and His grace for the needs of the Church in our time. —Pope Pius XII

PRAYER. *As You showed St. Margaret Mary the greatness of Your love, Lord Jesus, so now reveal Your love to me. Let me know with certainty that You are Love Incarnate, and all You wish of me is to live in Your love.*

BLESSED are you among women and blessed is the fruit of your womb! **MAY 16**

—Lk 2:42

REFLECTION. How sweet, how consoling it is for us who wish to walk in the footsteps of the Lord to have before us Mary, her image, her remembrance, her kindness, her humility and purity, her greatness.

How close to us the Gospel is in the power that Mary personifies and radiates with human and superhuman splendor. —*Pope Paul VI*

PRAYER. *Mary, Mother and Model of the Church, pray for me. Guide me, protect me, console me, and teach me the ways of Your Son.*

WHEN you come to serve the Lord, prepare yourself for trials. Be sincere of heart and steadfast. **MAY 17**

—Sir 2:2

REFLECTION. The fundamental lesson of humility is that it neither wipes away the greatness of Christ nor reduces to nothingness our poor merit.

Humility is a moral attitude that does not destroy the values to which it is applied; it is a way to recognize and regain them. —*Pope Paul VI*

PRAYER. *Lord Jesus, You humbled Yourself in taking our flesh upon Yourself, and especially in dying upon the Cross. Teach me humility, so that my actions and words may always be filled with Your love.*

I WILL ask the Father and He will give you another Advocate to dwell with you forever, the Spirit of truth.

—Jn 14:16-17

REFLECTION. Christ did not found an abstract religion, a mere school of religious thought. He set up a community of apostles, of teachers, with the task of spreading His message and so giving rise to a society of believers: His Church.

He promised the Spirit of truth to His Church and then sent Him. —*Pope Paul VI*

PRAYER. *Lord Jesus, continue to send Your Spirit upon the Church. May I too hear Your call and follow You wherever You lead me.*

 MEN, amen, I say to you, if you ask the Father anything in My Name, He will give it to you.

—Jn 16:23

REFLECTION. Pray like Jesus. Pray intently. Pray today, always in the confident communion that prayer has established between us and the Father.

Because it is to a father, it is to the Father that our humble voice is addressed.

—*Pope Paul VI*

PRAYER. *Heavenly Father, I lift up my heart to You. I lift up my life to You. Entrust me in Your truth, so that I may conform my life entirely to Your will.*

FOR the Lord hears the poor, and He does not spurn His own who are in bonds. **MAY 20**

—Ps 69:34

REFLECTION. In the Divine Master's school we shall all remember to love poverty and the poor.

We shall love the poor in order to devote special interest to them, whether they be persons, classes, or nations in need of love and aid.

—*Pope Paul VI*

PRAYER. *Lord Jesus, You reached out to the poor in a special way, and You called them God's chosen ones. Grant me the grace to see the poor and needy with Your eyes and to love them with Your compassion.*

BUT I press on, hoping to lay hold of that for which Christ Jesus has laid hold of me. **MAY 21**

—Phil 3:12

REFLECTION. Whatever an individual person's journey of faith and acceptance of it, no one is passive.

Each one must work to improve the lot of others and thus make progress along the way of the Gospel.

—*Pope John Paul II*

PRAYER. *O Lord, teach me what I should do to further the spread of the Gospel. Let Your Spirit speak to my heart with words of wisdom and courage, and enable me to respond with great passion.*

AND the glory that You have given Me, I have given to them, that they may be one, even as We are.

MAY 22

—Jn 17:23

REFLECTION. The longing of Christ's Heart [that all be one] must be our invitation.

We must dedicate ourselves anew to the task of establishing among Catholics a firm and abiding love and witness to that unity which is the first mark of the Church.

—*Pope John XXIII*

PRAYER. *O Lord, let me be a source of unity in my own parish. Let me be an example of a willingness to forgive and to work with those who can at times be difficult.*

HOPING against hope, Abraham believed and he became the father of many nations.

MAY 23

—Rom 4:18

REFLECTION. Nourish your faith; faith in a just and merciful God, without Whom your life would be like a day without sun, a universe without light.

And faith in the Church, which, by the will of God, guides us with goodness and certainty to heaven. —*Pope John XXIII*

PRAYER. *O Lord, I need You, for without You I would be lost. And I need Your Church, for without her I would not know how to find You.*

YOU love justice and hate wickedness. Therefore God, your God, has anointed you with the oil of gladness.

MAY 24

—Ps 45:8

REFLECTION. Fortitude is a Christian virtue, the arduous and ever painful habit of rightful thinking; it is self-control and primacy of the spirit.

Fortitude is inseparable from the quest for, and the love of, truth, justice, and equity.

—Pope John XXIII

PRAYER. *Come, Holy Spirit, grant me Your many gifts. Today, in a special way I pray for the gift of fortitude. Grant me rightful thinking and self-control.*

MIND the things that are above, not the things that are on earth.

MAY 25

—Col 3:2

REFLECTION. Christianity is the meeting point of earth and heaven. It lays claim to the whole person, body and soul, intellect and will.

It calls people to raise their minds above the changing conditions of this earthly existence and reach upward for the eternal life of heaven.

—Pope John XXIII

PRAYER. *O Lord, help me to always remember that my Faith is not simply a set of agreed upon beliefs. It is a truth that cuts to the marrow of my bones, a truth that must be lived every moment of my life.*

LEAVE your gift before the altar, and go first to be reconciled with your brother. **MAY 26**
—Mt 5:24

REFLECTION. One of the first good works that flows from faith is one that is so desperately needed in this place and everywhere.

It is the work of reconciliation: reconciliation with God and reconciliation with one another. —*Pope John Paul II*

PRAYER. *O Lord, pour Your peace into my heart that I may experience Your healing love. Let me share that love with those who are wounded and broken as a knowing and willing instrument of Your peace.*

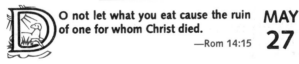 **D**O not let what you eat cause the ruin of one for whom Christ died. **MAY 27**
—Rom 14:15

REFLECTION. We cannot shut ourselves off within the narrow vision of our own interests, even sacred ones.

For we know that our brothers and sisters in faith throughout the whole world are facing the same problems as we are and perhaps without the means and resources that the Lord has given to us. —*Pope John XXIII*

PRAYER. *Remind me, O Lord, that I am not an island. Teach me to reach out in compassion to those who are suffering and in need of my love.*

N O one can lay a foundation other than the one that has been laid, namely Jesus Christ.

—1 Cor 3:11

REFLECTION. No matter how much we try, only through Jesus Christ shall we succeed in calling people back to the Majesty and Kingdom of God.

"No one," the Apostle admonishes us, "can lay a foundation other than the one that has been laid, namely Jesus Christ." —*Pope Pius X*

PRAYER. *Lord Jesus, truly You are my God and my All. Let me ever cling to You as the true foundation of my life and work, successes and failures, joys and sorrows.*

———

R ECEIVE the Holy Spirit; whose sins you shall forgive, they are forgiven.

—Jn 20:22-23

REFLECTION. The Sacrament of mercy and of forgiveness has to be lived out with a feeling of great confidence in Divine salvation and a sincere desire for conversion.

We must seek in it reconciliaton with God and with our brothers and sisters.

—*Pope John Paul II*

PRAYER. *O Lord, help me to appreciate the Sacrament of Reconciliation for the powerful gift it is. Teach me to avail myself of the Sacrament often and to invite others to share in the peace that I find in it.*

I DIRECTED my soul to wisdom, and in purity I found her. With her I gained understanding from the first.

MAY 30

—Sir 51:20

REFLECTION. Ideals, if they are authentic, if they are human, are not dreams: they are duties, especially for us Christians.

The more the sounds of the storm disturb the horizon of our history, the more such ideals must grip our attention. And ideals are energies; they are hopes. —*Pope Paul VI*

PRAYER. *Help me never to become so cynical, O Lord, that I stop dreaming. Let me never stop aiming for my ideals, even when I know that I might fall short.*

 EHOLD, henceforth all generations shall call me blessed, because He Who is mighty has done great things for me.

MAY 31

—Lk 1:48-49

REFLECTION. More than any other person, Mary was aware of God's love for her, of all the great things the Lord has done for her.

Mary's life was a response to God's love.

—*Pope John Paul II*

PRAYER. *Heavenly Father, Mary's response to Your call to be the Mother of Your Son was one of great generosity. Teach me that same generosity. Like Mary, may I think more of the need of others than of my own convenience.*

OME to Me heedfully, listen that you may have life. I will renew with you the eternal Covenant.

JUNE 1

—Is 55:3

REFLECTION. The attitude of the human person in the quest for truth is already an act of praise of the Author of truth.

It is the Author of truth Who alone can fully satisfy the human intellect.

—*Pope John Paul II*

PRAYER. *God of Wisdom, when I was small, I would ask questions about why things were the way they were. Teach me to continue to ask these questions, for they are certain to lead me to You.*

O not deceive yourselves. If you think you are wise in this world, you should become fools so as to be wise.

JUNE 2

—1 Cor 3:18

REFLECTION. Christians today, like Christians during the first centuries, must have courage and faith in God. They must distinguish themselves from the world about them.

They do this not to condemn the world but to penetrate it with the light and truth of the Gospel.

—*Pope John Paul II*

PRAYER. *O Lord, give me the courage that You gave to the Martyrs of the early Church. Help me to show that courage in my everyday life.*

CHASTISED a little, they shall be greatly blessed, because God tried them and found them worthy of Himself.

JUNE 3

—Wis 3:5

REFLECTION. From Jesus' behavior we learn a double lesson: that human suffering has a precise role to play in God's plan, and that it moves to compassion the Heart of Jesus.

For He knows how much suffering can affect human weakness and put it to the test.

—*Pope John Paul II*

PRAYER. *Almighty God, St. Charles Lwanga and his companions were tried in the crucible of suffering and found worthy. May I be willing to see Your will in my suffering.*

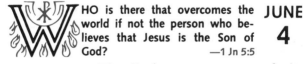

WHO is there that overcomes the world if not the person who believes that Jesus is the Son of God?

JUNE 4

—1 Jn 5:5

REFLECTION. The Savior expects great fruits from us, and we can supply them in ever greater measure.

However, this is true only if we remain in Him, bathed in His Most Precious Blood and inflamed by the fire of His love.

—*Pope John XXIII*

PRAYER. *Bathe me in Your love, O Lord. Enkindle the fire of my love. Let our love be one, and may that love heal a broken world.*

HOW beautiful are the feet of those who preach the Gospel of peace, of those who bring glad tidings of good things! —Rom 10:15

REFLECTION. We must conform our lives to the Gospel in all its fullness, accepting its demands and trusting its wisdom.

Then despite the skepticism of some and the ridicule of others, we shall be drawing many people to Christ. —*Pope John Paul II*

PRAYER. *O Lord, St. Boniface proclaimed the Gospel to the peoples of Germany. Help me to witness to the Faith in the small ways in which I allow Your Gospel to penetrate my every word and action.*

JESUS said to them, "Come apart to a quiet place and rest a while." —Mk 6:31

REFLECTION. Silence is the vital space dedicated to the Lord, in an atmosphere of listening and assimilation of His Word.

To remain faithful and zealous, it is necessary to know how to receive the Divine inspirations that come interiorly.

—*Pope John Paul II*

PRAYER. *O Lord, teach me to escape from the busy-ness of life to find a quiet place in which I can converse with You.*

FEAR not, for I have redeemed you. I have called you by name.

JUNE 7

—Is 43:1

REFLECTION. Listen to the voices that call you to great things.

They call you to your individual work, honestly and humbly performed; to a right conception of social service; and to a true witness each day of your lives by holiness and sanctity. —*Pope John XXIII*

PRAYER. *O Lord, give me the grace to do well those things that I have been called to do. Let me see in this the very dawning of the Kingdom.*

WE do not live for ourselves alone; neither do we die for ourselves alone.

JUNE 8

—Rom 14:7

REFLECTION. Today it is necessary for us to adopt environmental decisions.

These must also take into account the moral responsibility that we bear toward future generations. —*Pope John Paul II*

PRAYER. *Let me remember, O Lord, that every time I recycle paper, aluminum, glass, and plastic, every time I save water or electric power, every time I plant a tree, I am celebrating the gift of Your creation and preserving the world for generations to come.*

EACH me to do Your will, for You are my God. May Your good Spirit lead me on a level path.

JUNE 9

—Ps 143:10

REFLECTION. The spiritual life embraces many efforts, many forms of prayer, the Sacraments, asceticism, many exercises, but the essence is always the same.

It is the meeting of the Holy Spirit with the human spirit, the door of the human spirit open to the Divine Spirit. *—Pope John Paul II*

PRAYER. *Come, Holy Spirit! Descend upon me and inflame my heart with Your love. As You are the Love between the Father and the Son, so now be the Love that unites me with Them.*

———————

 O not judge, that you may not be judged. For with what judgment you judge, you shall be judged.

JUNE 10

—Mt 7:1-2

REFLECTION. The real Church is being born today in the faithfulness and boldness of the Spirit, in the unity of Christ's Body. We do not ask you to praise her a priori, but to give these positive facts the place they deserve.

Like the Lord, we say to you: Come and see.

—Pope Paul VI

PRAYER. *O Lord, let me never prejudge actions of the Church that might seem questionable. Let me find love in her and love her into healing.*

N hearing it, many of His disciples said, "This is a hard saying; who can accept it?"

—Jn 6:60

JUNE 11

REFLECTION. The demands Jesus makes upon His followers are not empty rhetoric, and they do not change with the passing of time. He calls us to conversion, to reconciliation with God and one another.

Jesus wishes us to hear the "hard sayings" as well as the words of confidence and encouragement. —*Pope John Paul II*

PRAYER. *Open my heart to conversion, O Lord, so that I may hear not only what I want to hear but also, and especially, what I need to hear.*

 E kind and compassionate to one another, forgiving one another, just as in Christ God forgave you.

-—Eph 4:32

JUNE 12

REFLECTION. Anyone who enters the Church enters an atmosphere of love. Let no one say, "I am a stranger here."

Let everyone say, "This is my home. I am in the Church. I am in charity. Here I am loved." —*Pope Paul VI*

PRAYER. *O Lord, let my parish family be truly a family. May all the members, including myself, be welcoming, interested in each other, and caring, especially toward those who have the least to give in return.*

THOSE who eat My Flesh and drink My Blood abide in Me, and I in them.
—Jn 6:56

REFLECTION. The love that comes from the Eucharist is a love that radiates in the fusion of hearts, in affection, in union, in forgiveness.

It makes us see that we have to spend ourselves for the sake of others, for the little ones, the poor, the sick, prisoners, exiles, the suffering. —*Pope Paul VI*

PRAYER. *O Lord, St. Anthony of Padua had a deep devotion to the Eucharist. May my Communion lead me to be bread that is broken to feed the hunger of a world starving for love.*

WHAT do you have that you have not received? And if you have received it, why do you boast as if you did not? —1 Cor 4:7

REFLECTION. An apostle who wants to be yeast for society must follow the most necessary precondition for yeast to be effective.

Such an apostle must take care to remain part of the mass.

—*Pope Paul VI*

PRAYER. *O Lord, may I never allow myself to feel superior to others. Let me always remember that the gifts You have bestowed upon me are gifts to be shared and not riches to be possessed.*

HOSE who are faithful in a very small matter are also faithful in great matters.

—Lk 10:16

REFLECTION. Faithfulness is the reason for living. It is not a chain restraining the boldness of talent and love.

When it consists of adherence to our creed, which never ages and never is exhausted, it opens a path to order, always positive, strong, and happy. —*Pope Paul VI*

PRAYER. *Lord Jesus, help me never to see my commitment to my Faith as a prison. On the contrary, let me regard it as a suitable means of expressing my life and my love.*

HEN I am lifted up from the earth, I will draw all things to Myself.

—Jn 12:32

REFLECTION. It could be said that the Cross, its awful scene, its shameful story, would create an emptiness around itself, would repel the contemplation of humans. Instead, however, the Cross attracts.

Jesus Himself predicted it: "When I am lifted up from the earth, I will draw all things to Myself." —*Pope Paul VI*

PRAYER. *Lead me to Your Cross, Lord Jesus. May I die for love of You Who have died for love of me.*

E said to them, "Go you also and work in My vineyard, and I will give you whatever is just."

JUNE 17

—Mt 20:4

REFLECTION. Hear the voice of Christ, calling you to join His workers: invest life with a direction, by making your own the concern of the Church for the elevation and progress of people.

The Church fully understands the yearnings of your generous heart.

—*Pope Paul VI*

PRAYER. *Here I am, O Lord; I wish to do Your will. Grant me the strength to surrender my life, my love, my all to You.*

LOVE You, O Lord, my strength. The Lord is my rock, my fortress, my deliverer.

JUNE 18

—Ps 18:2

REFLECTION. Love alone makes Jesus the Savior. Only through the ways of love can we approach Him, imitate Him, and bring Him into our souls.

Only through the ways of love can we bring Him into the ever dramatic vicissitudes of human history. —*Pope Paul VI*

PRAYER. *Love is such an overused word, O Lord, and sometimes it is difficult to know what loving You means. Teach me Your ways of love, the true love that only You can give.*

Y day I cry out; at night I clamor in Your presence. May my prayer come before You.

—Ps 88:2-3

REFLECTION. Prayer is able to transform the world. Everything is new with prayer, both for individuals and for communities.

New goals and new ideals emerge. Christian dignity and action are reaffirmed.

—*Pope John Paul II*

PRAYER. *Lord Jesus, You said that if we ask anything in Your Name, it will be granted. I ask You, now, to teach me to pray. Help me to remember that prayer is the most important thing I can do.*

———

ITH an everlasting love I have loved you; therefore, I have kept My mercy toward you.

—Jer 31:3

REFLECTION. Our world is suffering in the icy grip of selfishness and fever.

It needs to feel the certainty that renews and confirms forever the great work of the Covenant: "The Lord chooses you, the Lord loves you." —*Pope Paul VI*

PRAYER. *O Lord, You have loved me with a love that has healed me and taught me to love You and myself. I promise to share that love with all those who are trapped in loneliness and self-hate.*

AY to those with fearful hearts, "Take courage, do not be afraid. Behold, your God will ... save you."

JUNE 21

—Is 35:4

REFLECTION. To construct this world you have to undertake great tasks. If you want your legitimate ideals to be meaningful and not halfhearted, beginning now you must be daring, patient, and sincere with yourselves.

You must also have an unshakable faith.

—*Pope John Paul II*

PRAYER. *Awaken my faith, O Lord, so that I may renew my commitment to You. Let me give myself totally to building Your Kingdom upon this earth by everything I say and do.*

WORE my righteousness like a garment; justice was my robe and my turban.

JUNE 22

—Job 29:14

REFLECTION. In the present-day confusion of the notion of good and evil, licit and illicit, just and unjust, in the demoralizing spread of crime and immorality, we will do well to preserve and deepen the sense of natural law.

This means the sense of justice, of integrity, and of the good. —*Pope Paul VI*

PRAYER. *O Lord, help me never to lose a sense of what is right and just. Let me never be deceived by the conflicting voices of a confused world, but always seek and live Your truth.*

LET there be no dissensions among you, but be perfectly united in one mind and in one judgment.

JUNE 23

—1 Cor 1:10

REFLECTION. Nothing is so inconsistent with the Church of Jesus Christ as division; nothing is so opposed to her very life as for her members to take refuge in selfish solitude.

There is nothing worse than for them to be too much devoted to themselves and to take an interest only in the private concerns of their own little group. —*Pope Pius XII*

PRAYER. *Widen my horizons, O Lord, to the needs of those around me. May I learn to share their joys and sorrows, their hopes and fears.*

 AS it is written in Isaiah the Prophet, "Prepare the way of the Lord, make straight His paths."

JUNE 24

—Mk 1:2-3

REFLECTION. An unexpected child, St. John the Baptist, called out to the people.

He told them to prepare for a heavenly announcement, an invitation to universal rebirth.

—*Pope John XXIII*

PRAYER. *Heavenly Father, may my words and my actions proclaim to others that today is the day to prepare the way for the Lord. Everyday is the day to welcome the Church's Bridegroom.*

Y Word that goes forth from My mouth will not return to Me void but will accomplish what I desire.

—Is 55:11

REFLECTION. The history of the human race in the world is not a procession of blind forces. It is a marvelous and vital working out of the actual history of the Divine Word.

From Him came its first movements and through Him it will reach fulfillment.

—*Pope Pius XII*

PRAYER. *It has been said, O Lord, that those in love with God will realize that their lives are a part of a Divine conspiracy. Help me to recognize the action of Your love in my life.*

 HRIST is faithful as the Son over His own house. We are that house if we hold on to our courage and our hope.

JUNE 26

—Heb 3:6

REFLECTION. Jesus became a baby, He became poor, He became a victim, so that no one might feel that He was above or distant; He placed Himself at the feet of all.

Jesus is for all, He belongs to all, and indeed to each of us individually.   —*Pope Paul VI*

PRAYER. *Lord Jesus, it is so easy to forget how much I mean to You and how much You should mean to me. Remind me that I am precious to You, and help me to make You the center of my life.*

BEYOND all question, great is the mystery of godliness.

—1 Tim 3:16

REFLECTION. Our religion, which is truth, is Divine reality in human history. It cannot be discovered or invented.

It is received and, ancient though it is, it is always alive, always new. —*Pope Paul VI*

PRAYER. *O Lord, teach me Your Word, Your Will, Your Truth. Enable me to learn more about my Faith. But help me also to have the humility to realize that after I have studied all my life, I will have just begun to touch the Mystery.*

YOUR Word is a lamp to my feet and a light for my path.

—Ps 119:105

REFLECTION. When the Church assembles in prayer to reflect on the Word of God, the Holy Spirit Himself pours out God's love on His people.

He gives them the hope that does not disappoint. —*Pope John Paul II*

PRAYER. *O Lord, You breathed Your Spirit into the hearts of the sacred authors. Breathe that same Spirit into my heart, so that as I read and study Holy Scripture, I may recognize it as Your loving Word spoken to humankind.*

JESUS saw Simon and Andrew.... "Come, follow Me," He said, "and I will make you fish for people."

JUNE 29

—Mk 1:16-17

REFLECTION. Neither success nor failure must ever cause you to forget your vocation as servant. Allow the Lord to grant growth when and how He chooses.

At the same time, imitate the Apostle Paul who knew how to suffer want and to live in abundance, ready for anything.—*Pope John Paul II*

PRAYER. *Lord Jesus, You called St. Peter by the Sea of Galilee and St. Paul on the road to Damascus. Call me again and entrust Your sacred mission into my hands.*

I CAN do all things in Him Who strengthens me.

JUNE 30

—Phil 4:13

REFLECTION. Remember how the first Christians, most of them simple and humble people, suffering the most cruel persecutions, were successful in spreading Christ's message to all parts of the empire.

Their only weapons were prayer, the Gospel, and the Cross. —*Pope John Paul II*

PRAYER. *O Lord, the First Martyrs of Rome were not rich or wise, but You filled them with Your riches, Your wisdom. Fill me, too, with Your gifts, for without You I can do nothing.*

WHO is weak, and I do not feel weak? Who is led into sin, and I am not indignant?

JULY 1

—2 Cor 11:29

REFLECTION. Do not remain passive when the dignity and honor of the human person are threatened.

This threat is due to violence, economic exploitation, and the decay of morals, of which our permissive society too often gives a sorry display. —*Pope Paul VI*

PRAYER. *O Lord, give me a discerning heart and a courageous spirit. Let me fight for the dignity of all, especially those who are most defenseless and vulnerable in our society.*

STRIVE to enter by the narrow gate; for many, I tell you, will seek to enter and will not be able.

JULY 2

—Lk 13:24

REFLECTION. Let no one be under any delusion. Christ is demanding. Christ's life is the narrow way. To be worthy of Him, we must take up our cross.

It is not enough to be religious; it is necessary to carry out the Divine Will in actual fact. —*Pope Paul VI*

PRAYER. *Give me the courage to take the narrow path that leads to You, Lord Jesus. Let me always remember that following You means not only saying "Yes" to Your love but also "No" to the things opposed to Your love.*

EARN not the ways of the nations, and have no fear of the signs of the heavens.

—Jer 10:2

REFLECTION. Christ belongs to you! Do not be afraid anymore—not even of the Cross, His Cross that He will share with you. The royal triumph of Jesus leads to the Cross.

But, we repeat, do not be afraid: in this way life, true life will be assured for you tomorrow.

—*Pope Paul VI*

PRAYER. *Calm my fears, O Lord, and relieve my anxiety. Let me place all my hopes in You. And when the storms threaten, assure me that You will guide me safely home.*

OR the Father Himself loves you because you have loved Me and have believed that I came forth from God.

—Jn 16:27

REFLECTION. A man and a woman who love each other, the smile of a child, peace in the home: a sermon without words, but so wonderfully convincing.

In them everyone can glimpse, as through a transparency, the reflection of another love and its infinite call.

—*Pope Paul VI*

PRAYER. *Heavenly Father, let me see Your presence in the everyday events of my life. May I recognize that these small things are really miracles of Your love.*

E renewed in the spirit of your mind and put on the new self, created according to God in justice and holiness of truth.

JULY 5

—Eph 4:23

REFLECTION. Do not be intimidated by anything because God is our hope. Fight, with eagerness and courage, the battle of love.

This battle begins in yourselves and in your families, with the removal of selfishness and misunderstandings and a striving to drown evil in an abundance of God. —*Pope John Paul II*

PRAYER. *Lord God, fill me with Your hope. Remind me that I can help change the world, especially if I start by trying to change my own heart.*

O I say: Walk in the Spirit, and you will not gratify the desires of the sinful nature.

JULY 6

—Gal 5:17

REFLECTION. One of the underlying problems today is a loss of appreciation of the virtue of chastity. How important it is to recover this virtue in our own time!

Chastity helps us to harmonize all the dimensions of our sexuality and thus to live joyfully in accordance with God's will.

—*Pope John Paul II*

PRAYER. *Lord Jesus, in a world obsessed with sex, it is so easy to lose perspective. Give me the courage to live a life that is chaste, after the example of St. Maria Goretti.*

YOU have been called to liberty, brothers and sisters; only do not use liberty as an occasion for sensuality.

—Gal 5:13

REFLECTION. Liberty and authority are not opposing terms, but values that complement each other.

Their mutual cooperation fosters growth of the community and of the capacities for initiative and enrichment of individual values.

—*Pope Paul VI*

PRAYER. *Heavenly Father, teach me to cherish the freedom that is Your gift, a freedom that is not afraid to commit itself to love or to obey authority.*

LET us consider how we spur one another toward charity and good works.

—Heb 10:24

REFLECTION. Charity! Charity! Is this your hour? Let us all try to be worthy of her and prepare her ways.

Let us pray, let us love, let us work so that our charity may be in our hearts and may be able to work the wonder of her triumph. —*Pope Paul VI*

PRAYER. *O Lord, let there be an explosion of Your love in our land. There are so many who are lonely, so many trapped in guilt and self-hate. There is so much violence and selfishness. Help me to work and pray to make this a better place.*

GOD does great things beyond our knowing; wonders past our searching out.

—Job 37:5

REFLECTION. God is present, no matter how often humanity may forget God.

Christianity has the living and modern spiritual energy, ready to confront the negations of a materialistic world.

—*Pope John XXIII*

PRAYER. *O Lord, when I listen to the news, I begin to wonder why You allow all of this to happen. Enable me to be aware of Your Presence more clearly, and let me work ever harder to be a sign of Your Presence.*

KEEP your lips from speaking deceit. Depart from evil, and do good. Seek peace and pursue it.

—Ps 34:13-14

REFLECTION. There can be no outward peace unless it reflects and is ruled by that interior peace without which the affairs of human beings shake, totter, and fall.

Only God's holy religion can foster, strengthen, and maintain such a peace.

—*Pope John XXIII*

PRAYER. *Help me to find peace in my heart, O Lord. Teach me to turn things over to Your care; enable me to surrender to Your will in all things.*

AY the gracious care of the Lord our God rest upon us and prosper the work of our hands.

JULY 11

—Ps 90:17

REFLECTION. Work is a fundamental part of our earthly life. It often involves heavy fatigue and even suffering, but it can also forge strong character and vigorous personality.

It can be the means by which we build up the world according to the values in which we believe. —*Pope John Paul II*

PRAYER. *O Lord, St. Benedict taught that "to work is to pray." Help me to discern Your Presence in my workplace and bear witness to Your love to my coworkers.*

 OW it came to pass that Jesus went out into the hills to pray, and he continued all night in prayer.

JULY 12

—Lk 6:12

REFLECTION. Sometimes, in the anxiety of our modern mentality to get things done, we are inclined to consider prayer as an obstacle to action, as if they were competing for time.

In fact, action and prayer must be complementary. —*Pope Paul VI*

PRAYER. *Lord Jesus, You spent whole nights in prayer. Help me to find those moments of silence during which I can regain perspective and receive again the strength to do Your work.*

ITH all prayer and supplication pray at all times in the Spirit.... Always keep on praying for all the saints. —Eph 6:18

REFLECTION. The Christian will for peace has its weapons too.

Its principal arms are those of prayer and love: constant prayer to the Father of Heaven; brotherly love among all, since all are children of the same Father. —Pope Pius XII

PRAYER. *O Lord, help me to remember that prayer changes reality. Enable me to believe that my prayers are the most important way I can heal broken hearts and change a broken world.*

 HE centurion said, "Lord, my servant is lying at home sick...." Jesus replied, "I will come and heal him." —Mt 8:6-7

REFLECTION. One of the most striking aspects of the public ministry of Jesus was His special love for those who were suffering.

He touched, blessed, and healed them. He forgave their sins. He offered them consolation and hope by proclaiming to them the Gospel of salvation. —Pope John Paul II

PRAYER. *Grant me Your compassion, Lord Jesus. Help me to reach out to the weak and humble people in my life, especially those whom I have often overlooked or even ignored.*

TRIVE for peace with everyone and that holiness without which no one will see God. —Heb 12:14

JULY 15

REFLECTION. Holiness reveals itself in the last analysis as fullness of life, boundless happiness, and immersion in the light of Christ and God.

It is also an inebriating foretaste of the Communion of Saints, that is, of the living Church who is the Lord's, both in time and in eternity. —*Pope Paul VI*

PRAYER. *O Lord, let me be one with You, Who are threefold holy. Grant me Your grace and Your holiness.*

 AILY I was the Lord's delight, rejoicing before Him always, rejoicing in His inhabited world and delighting in the human race. —Prov 8:30-31

JULY 16

REFLECTION. Mother of the incarnate Word! You are the human heart's immaculate sensitivity to all that is of God.

This means all that is true, good, and beautiful, all that has its source and fulfillment in God. —*Pope John Paul II*

PRAYER. *Blessed Virgin Mary, intercede for me so that I may view the world with your eyes of love. Grant that I may always give witness to the goodness of God by following your example of generosity.*

I HAVE set before you life and death.... Choose life, that you and your descendants may live.

JULY 17

—Dt 30:19

REFLECTION. Be the defenders of human life, whenever it is threatened.

Be such particularly of those who are helpless, or when recourse to war does not seem justified by an absolute necessity of justice.

—*Pope Paul VI*

PRAYER. *Heavenly Father, You have given us such a wonderful gift in human life. May I always defend the right to life, especially for the vulnerable, and cherish the gift of life I have received.*

———————

 J ESUS asked them, "When I sent you out without purse, bag, or sandals, did you lack anything?" They said, "Nothing."

JULY 18

—Lk 22:35-36

REFLECTION. The world expects from us simplicity of life, the spirit of prayer, charity to all, especially the lowly and poor, obedience, humility, detachment, and self-sacrifice.

Without this mark of holiness, our word will have difficulty in touching the hearts of people today. —*Pope Paul VI*

PRAYER. *Lord Jesus, I promise today to examine my life in light of the call to Gospel simplicity. I promise to try to simplify my life in any way that I can.*

O not be wise in your own eyes. Fear the Lord and turn away from evil.

—Prov 3:7

REFLECTION. If fear of God is taken away from the soul, the word holiness, the supreme perfection of our being, no longer has any meaning.

In addition, the word sin, which is an absurd violation of Divine Law, no longer has any meaning. —*Pope Paul VI*

PRAYER. *O Lord, in the face of Your overwhelming good, I recognize my own unworthiness. I am a sinner. Forgive me, and let me once again walk in Your love.*

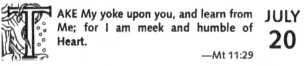 AKE My yoke upon you, and learn from Me; for I am meek and humble of Heart.

—Mt 11:29

REFLECTION. How do we picture Christ? What does Jesus seem to be like at first sight? Once again, His own words help us. He said, "I am meek and humble of Heart."

This is how Jesus wishes to be seen.

—*Pope Paul VI*

PRAYER. *Lord Jesus, teach me to take Your yoke upon me and learn from You, so that I may rest in You. Let me turn my difficulties and anxieties over to You, knowing that in You all things will work out for the best.*

ESUS said to the lawyer, "You have answered correctly. Do this and you will live."

—Lk 10:28

JULY 21

REFLECTION. Christians must restore their spiritual and moral unity. It is not enough to say we are Christians. We must live as Christians.

Genuine Christians derive the rule, style, and strength of their life from the Faith.

—*Pope Paul VI*

PRAYER. *O Lord, let me find a consistency between my beliefs and my actions. May all who see me know that I have committed myself to You with heart, mind, and soul.*

UR present light afflictions, which are for the moment, are achieving for us an eternal glory that is beyond all measure. —2 Cor 4:17

JULY 22

REFLECTION. Someone would have a poor idea of human and marital love by thinking that affection and joy vanish when difficulties come. This is when we really see what motivates people.

Here also is where gift and tenderness are consolidated, because true love does not think about itself, but about how to increase the good of the beloved. —*Pope John Paul II*

PRAYER. *O Lord, teach me to see beyond the difficulties of the present moment. Let me realize that these moments of trial are also opportunities to show a greater love.*

SK, and it will be given you. Seek, and you will find. Knock, and it will be opened to you.

—Mt 7:7

REFLECTION. In prayer we seek, find, and converse with God just as we would with an intimate friend.

We can speak of our sorrows and joys, our weaknesses and problems, and our desires to be better and to help others to be better too.

—Pope John Paul II

PRAYER. *Dear Lord, guard me from the danger of saying to You what I think You want to hear. Teach me to pray in such a way that I truly express that which is in my heart and mind.*

IGHT the good fight of the faith. Take hold of the life eternal to which you have been called.

—1 Tim 6:12

REFLECTION. Strong in faith, put up a good fight; the future belongs to the believers and not to the skeptics and doubters. The future belongs to those who love, not to those who hate.

The Church's mission in the world, far from being ended or outmoded, goes out to meet new trials and fresh enterprises. —Pope Pius XII

PRAYER. *Teach me to trust, O Lord, that You guide the Church through the action of the Holy Spirit. Let me believe with all my heart that she will be victorious.*

EVERYONE who has left house, or [family] ... or lands for My Name's sake, shall receive a hundredfold and shall possess life everlasting. —Mt 19:29

JULY 25

REFLECTION. The coming of the Holy Spirit does not take the Cross away from human reality.

It is not a talisman that immunizes human life from sufferings and misfortunes. —*Pope Paul VI*

PRAYER. *Lord Jesus, You promised those who follow You a reward of a hundredfold. Yet so many who have committed themselves to You, like St. James the Greater, have suffered greatly. Help me to understand the meaning of the Cross You share with us.*

LISTEN to your father, who gave you life, and despise not your mother when she is old. —Prov 23:22

JULY 26

REFLECTION. Heat and food are not enough; there is also the heart; we must think of the heart of our old people.

The Lord said that parents must be respected and loved, even when they are old.

—*Pope John Paul I*

PRAYER. *Lord God, thank You for the wonderful gift of my parents. Let me always honor them—with love and care while they are alive and with my prayers when they have returned to You.*

OU have received a Spirit of adoption as children, by virtue of which we cry "Abba!" "Father!"

JULY 27

—Rom 8:16

REFLECTION. If the Church is able to enter a preparation for the perennial coming of the Holy Spirit, He, the "Light of hearts," will not hesitate to come.

He will give Himself for the joy, the light, the fortitude, the apostolic virtue, and the unitive charity that the Church needs today.

—Pope Paul VI

PRAYER. *Come, Holy Spirit, into my heart. Set the world on fire with Your love. Give me the courage to be what I am called to be.*

HE life that I live now in the flesh, I live in the faith of the Son of God. He loved me and gave Himself up for me.

JULY 28

—Gal 2:20

REFLECTION. The Eucharist is the privileged summit of the meeting of Christ's love for us; a love that is made available for each of us, a love that is made to be sacrificial lamb and food for our hunger for life.

As the Apostle says, "He loved me and gave Himself up for me." —Pope Paul VI

PRAYER. *Fill me with gratitude, O Lord, every time I participate in the Eucharist. May I be conscious of its meaning, that it is a powerful sign of Your love for me.*

YOU are My friends if you do the things I command you.

—Jn 15:14

REFLECTION. Lord Jesus, grant that those You have called Your friends may come to know in fullness the joy You have promised.

May they know the joy of praising You, the joy of serving their brothers and sisters, the joy of abiding in Your love. —*Pope John Paul II*

PRAYER. *Lord Jesus, You taught St. Martha a lesson in the true meaning of love. Help me to realize that You have called me to be Your friend and enable me to respond to that call with all my heart, soul, and strength.*

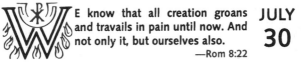

WE know that all creation groans and travails in pain until now. And not only it, but ourselves also.

—Rom 8:22

REFLECTION. If humanity "groans and travails in pain," it does so to the extent that people's minds and hearts are not lifted up with Christ to God.

Their consciences are not conformed through Christ to the wisdom that comes from God. —*Pope John Paul II*

PRAYER. *O Lord, send Your Spirit into my heart so that my every thought may conform to Your will and my every action give witness to Your love.*

JUST as Christ has arisen from the dead through the glory of the Father, so we also may walk in newness of life.

JULY
31

—Rom 6:4

REFLECTION. Do not make concessions as regards truth and goodness. Do not stoop to compromise on the Gospel values that must be the basis of your life.

For they are the foundation of your new life inaugurated by Christ.

—*Pope John Paul II*

PRAYER. *Send Your Spirit of truth into my heart, O Almighty God, so that I may remain faithful to Your Word daily in my every speech and action.*

PAUL stood up in the midst of the Areopagus and said, "... What you worship in ignorance, that I proclaim to you."

AUG.
1

—Acts 17:22-23

REFLECTION. Catholics must become closer to the "unchurched" and help them discover their true vocation in Christ.

This is the best service we can render to them and the best expression of solidarity and friendship.

—*Pope John Paul II*

PRAYER. *O Lord, grant me the courage to share my Faith with others. May I never be embarrassed by the fact that I am Catholic, but rather seek to share my Faith with everyone I meet.*

ESUS said to Martha, "Did I not tell you that if you believe you will behold the glory of God?"

AUG.
2

—Lk 11:40

REFLECTION. We must be open, listen, seek to understand. We must go beyond the limits, because all that is Divine, that is revealed, is superior to the human, to our limits.

Many people do not accept it because they do not see or because they cannot go beyond these limits. —*Pope John Paul II*

PRAYER. *It is so easy to become trapped in my own little world, O Lord. Help me to be ready to accept with humility that which is Mystery and beyond my comprehension.*

 F You my heart speaks; You my glance seeks; Your Presence, O Lord, I seek.

AUG.
3

—Ps 27:8

REFLECTION. In the light of faith, each one of you can look at others as if they were an icon, a portrait—at least a potential one—of Christ.
—*Pope John Paul II*

PRAYER. *Lord Jesus, let me treat each person whom I meet with sacred respect. Help me to see in them, and especially in those who are most lowly, Your presence, Your Face, Your Heart.*

IF we confess our sins, He is faithful and just to forgive us our sins and cleanse us from all iniquity.

AUG.
4

—1 Jn 1:9

REFLECTION. Confession is an act of honesty and courage; an act of entrusting ourselves, beyond sin, to a loving and forgiving God.

It is an act of the prodigal son who returns to his Father and is welcomed by Him with the gift of peace. —*Pope John Paul II*

PRAYER. *Lord God, St. John Vianney spent much of his life listening to the confessions of the faithful. May his example teach me to rededicate myself to the reconciliation You are offering.*

GOD'S mercy extends from generation to generation to those who fear Him.

AUG.
5

—Lk 1:50

REFLECTION. In her *Magnificat*, which has become the canticle of the Church and of humanity yearning for salvation, Mary has proclaimed human and feminine liberation.

She is the most perfect image of freedom and of the liberation of humanity and of the universe.

—*Pope John Paul II*

PRAYER. *I thank You, O Lord, for You have offered me true liberation: the forgiveness of my sins and the healing of my weaknesses.*

AND as Jesus prayed, the appearance of His countenance was changed, and His raiment became white as snow.
—Lk 9:29

REFLECTION. Liberation and salvation, signs of the Kingdom of God, have both a physical and a spiritual dimension.

Two actions are characteristic of the mission Jesus fulfilled: healing and forgiving.

—*Pope John Paul II*

PRAYER. *Lord Jesus, help me to realize that Your Transfiguration on Mount Tabor is not an event that separates You from us. It is rather a sign of the glory of the Kingdom into which You have invited us.*

SINCE we are surrounded by such a great cloud of witnesses [the Saints], ... let us run with patience the race set before us.
—Heb 12:1

REFLECTION. Prayer opens the mind and heart to God. It deepens our longing for His Kingdom.

Prayer consciously links us to the Communion of Saints, who support us by their continual intercession. —*Pope John Paul II*

PRAYER. *In prayer, O Lord, we join our love to Your own eternal love. We also join in a community of praise, the Church of the living and of those who have preceded us into the fullness of the Kingdom. May this realization bring us great consolation.*

EPROVE, entreat, rebuke with all patience and teaching. For there will come a time when people will not put up with sound doctrine. —2 Tim 4:2b-3

AUG. 8

REFLECTION. Like Paul, Dominic teaches all knowledge and all virtue with authority, refutes doctrinal errors, stirs up and encourages what is good, reproves and corrects bad morals.

He does this always with unalterable patience and heavenly wisdom. —*Pope Pius XII*

PRAYER. *O Lord, I realize that part of a disciple's duty is to correct those who are in error. May I correct not because I am self-righteous, but more because I genuinely care for those who need my love.*

OD has revealed them to us through His Spirit. For the Spirit searches all things, even the deep things of God. —1 Cor 3:10

AUG. 9

REFLECTION. Every apostolate is an action of Christ Himself; it cannot be exercised except under the impulse of the Spirit. The Spirit searches out the deep things of God.

The Spirit also arouses in us an ineffable prayer and continues the salvific action of Christ through the Church's members.

—*Pope Paul VI*

PRAYER. *Lord Jesus, teach me to listen to the promptings of the Spirit and give me the love to respond to the Spirit's call with generosity.*

ESUS said, "I am the Way, and the Truth, and the Life. No one comes to the Father except through Me."

AUG.
10

—Jn 14:6

REFLECTION. Christ is absolute Truth; in Him the Father offers human beings the complete answer to all the questions that worry them.

In Christ we can discover the full truth about ourselves and about the world.

—*Pope John Paul II*

PRAYER. *O Lord, may I never seek any truth that is not based in You. Help me to reject those half-truths that are so popular today, but that do not lead to life. Let me bring my questions to You and Your Church.*

———————

 O creature will be able to separate us from the love of God, which is in Christ Jesus our Lord.

AUG.
11

—Rom 8:39

REFLECTION. In humanity beauty produces love; in Christ love precedes and produces the beauty of the Church, that is, the beauty of humanity loved and redeemed by Christ, and thus brought back to its original perfection.

The Church, ablaze with Christ's Spirit, is like a bright lamp. —*Pope Paul VI*

PRAYER. *Lord Jesus, St. Clare celebrated the love of God. Teach me to recognize Your love in nature, in people, in the Church, and in my own heart.*

HE publican ... kept striking his breast, saying, "O God, be merciful to me, a sinner." **AUG. 12**

—Lk 18:13

REFLECTION. Let us restore in ourselves the right awareness of sin, which is not frightening. The awareness of good will grows in opposition to the awareness of evil.

The sense of responsibility will grow, rising from inner moral judgment and widening to the sense of our duties, personal, social, and religious. —*Pope Paul VI*

PRAYER. *Lord Jesus, like the publican, I accuse myself of being a sinner. I have hurt myself and others by what I have done, and even more often, by what I have failed to do. Forgive me, O Lord.*

 ESUS went about ... curing every kind of disease and infirmity. And seeing the crowds, He had compassion on them. **AUG. 13**

—Mt 9:35-36

REFLECTION. Whenever you help a sick person, you are a sign of Christ's compassion for all who suffer. —*Pope John Paul II*

PRAYER. *Lord Jesus, You taught that whenever we do something for one of Your least ones, we are doing it for You. May I always reach out to those who need my help and my comfort.*

T O one He gave five talents, to another two, and to another one, to each according to his ability.

AUG.
14

—Mt 25:15

REFLECTION. You must trust in God, but also in yourselves.

You must trust in the admirable energies that God has given to every person for the development of personality and in a chosen form of life. —*Pope John XXIII*

PRAYER. *You have gifted me, O Lord, with many talents. May I recognize them and use them for my improvement and for the service of all.*

W HO is this that comes forth like the dawn, as beautiful as the moon, as resplendent as the sun?

AUG.
15

—Song 6:10

REFLECTION. On this feast of the glorious Assumption of Mary we celebrate the glorification of her immaculate soul and of her virginal body, of her perfect conformity to the risen Christ.

This is the same glorification and destiny of those whom Christ made His brothers and sisters. —*Pope Paul VI*

PRAYER. *Blessed Virgin Mary, intercede for your children. Teach me to follow the ways of your Son with ever greater devotion, and lead me home to heaven where you reign with your Son in glory.*

HOPE does not disappoint, because the charity of God is poured forth in our hearts by the Holy Spirit Who has been given to us. —Rom 5:5

AUG. 16

REFLECTION. The outpouring of the Spirit in our hearts brings about a change that is slow and hard won, but certain. It is a change that leads to the formation of the new person.

In this way, "we all attain to the unity of the faith and knowledge of the Son of God" (Eph 4:13). —*Pope Paul VI*

PRAYER. *Come, Holy Spirit, Creator blest; enter my heart with flames of Your love. Burn away all that is selfish, and purify all that is precious.*

JESUS went down to Nazareth with [His parents], and He was obedient to them. —Lk 2:51a

AUG. 17

REFLECTION. Extol the concept of the family, with consciousness of its being, its function, and its destiny, as a community of love, as the dispenser of God's creative power.

Extol it as the sign and the outpouring of the charity with which Christ loved and continues to love us. —*Pope Paul VI*

PRAYER. *O Lord, bless my family and protect all its members. Let it be the school at which we learn how to love each other as much as You have loved us.*

LET the word of Christ dwell in you abundantly, as you teach and admonish one another with all wisdom.

AUG. 18

—Col 3:16

REFLECTION. In the interior life we are not alone, but live with Christ.

We share His thoughts and actions, and we associate with Him as a friend, a disciple and, as it were, a collaborator. —*Pope Pius XII*

PRAYER. *Lord Jesus, whisper Your secrets into my heart. Teach me how to pray, how to meditate, how to be one with You.*

NOW that I, your Lord and Master, have washed your feet, you also ought to wash the feet of one another.

AUG. 19

—Jn 13:14

REFLECTION. What the world really asks of us is that the Mystery of Redemption be accessible to all, especially to the poor, the sick, children, the young, the family.

It is precisely through the Eucharist that Christ's Redemption touches each person's heart, transforming the world's history.

—*Pope John Paul II*

PRAYER. *When You washed the feet of Your disciples, Lord Jesus, You were proclaiming that the Eucharist is the sign of Your love for all. May my participation in the Eucharist make me willing to wash the feet of those who need my love.*

THE God of our fathers has appointed you beforehand to learn His will.
—Acts 22:14

REFLECTION. To discover the Lord's concrete will for us, we must listen to the Word of God, pray, and discuss our problems and discoveries with others.

In this way, we will discern the gifts we have received and use them profitably.

—*Pope John Paul II*

PRAYER. *O Lord, speak to me through Your Spirit-filled Word. Send brothers and sisters to help me discern Your will, and let me hear Your voice in the silence of my heart.*

GOD is love, and those who abide in love abide in God, and God in them.
—1 Jn 4:16

REFLECTION. Pius X knew no other road than the Eucharist by which he could arrive at heroism in his love of God.

He knew no other road by which he could return to the Redeemer of the world, Who by means of the Eucharist poured out the wealth of His Divine love on humans.   —*Pope Pius XII*

PRAYER. *Lord Jesus, increase my love for the Church and the Eucharist after the example of Pope St. Pius X. May it lead me to the sanctity we see in him.*

A GREAT sign appeared in the heavens: a woman clothed with the sun, and the moon was under her feet, and upon her head a crown of twelve stars. —Rev 12:1

AUG. 22

REFLECTION. Right from the first moment of her Divine Motherhood, of her union with the Son Whom the Father sent into the world, that the world might be saved through Him, Mary takes her place within Christ's Messianic service. —*Pope John Paul II*

PRAYER. *Mary, Mother of God, you are the Queen of the World and the Queen of Angels and Saints. Pray for me before the throne of your Son that I may remain close to Him in life and join Him in death.*

———————

D O not be overcome by evil, but overcome evil with good.
—Rom 12:21

AUG. 23

REFLECTION. Evil is not the only thing that is contagious; goodness is as well. It is necessary that, at this favorable hour, goodness increasingly abound in us!

Let us succumb to the contagion of goodness! —*Pope John Paul II*

PRAYER. *Let me do small acts of goodness to those around me, O Lord, even if they do not recognize what I am doing or why. Teach me to trust that You will bring these acts of goodness to fruition in Your own time.*

THEN said I, "Behold I come ... to do Your will, O God."

AUG. 24

—Heb 10:7

REFLECTION. I call. I call you. I know that this is bold of me, maybe even vain, possibly a bit inconvenient. But I must call out as Jesus did: come with me.

This is to ask for a precious gift, the gift of yourself to the Lord, a sacrifice without limitations.

—Pope Paul VI

PRAYER. *Here I am, O Lord. I have heard Your call and have come to do Your will. Take my life, my love, my all.*

WHEN you have done everything that was commanded you, say, "We are unprofitable servants."

AUG. 25

—Lk 18:10

REFLECTION. Christians should conscientiously take up their civic duties in a spirit of disinterested service.

This will lead them to renounce seeking their personal gain, power, or prestige, if it is harmful to others. —Pope Paul VI

PRAYER. *O Lord, grant me the generosity of spirit of St. Louis, the King. He served his country all his life; calling his fellow citizens to build a society based on Christ's teachings. Help me to do the same.*

VERY Scribe instructed in the Kingdom of heaven ... brings forth things new and old.

—Mt 13:52

REFLECTION. Hope, which is the gaze of the Church turned toward the future, fills her heart, and tells us how it is throbbing in new and loving expectation. The Church is not old, she is ancient.

Time does not subdue her; it rejuvenates her. —*Pope Paul VI*

PRAYER. *O Lord, in imitation of Your Church, let me never reject what is old simply because it is old. Teach me, like the good Scribe, to take and use the best of the old and the best of the new.*

 ET evildoers forsake their ways, and the wicked their thoughts, and let them return to the Lord.

—Is 55:7

REFLECTION. Change your thoughts, your tastes according to the will of God. Correct those faults that we often boast of as our principles and qualities. Search for a continual interior uprightness of feelings and resolutions.

Let yourselves really be guided by the love of God and by the love of your neighbor.

—*Pope Paul VI*

PRAYER. *O Lord, teach me to discern my intentions, sorting out what is selfish and base, building up what is loving and good.*

IN this we know that we love the children of God, when we love God and keep His commandments.

AUG. 28

—1 Jn 5:2

REFLECTION. We have our individual personal duty to be good. That does not mean to be weak. It means to be capable of breaking the sad logical chain of evil by patience and forgiveness.

It means to love, that is, to be Christians.

—*Pope Paul VI*

PRAYER. *Almighty God, St. Augustine taught that we should love You and do what we will. Let my love be real and profound so that whatever I do may truly be good and holy.*

JESUS said, "I have come to bring fire on the earth, and how I wish it were already kindled!"

AUG. 29

—Lk 12:49

REFLECTION. This is the flame that Jesus wanted to bring down upon the earth, the one He ardently desired to see enkindled: the fire of His charity, of the justice that He taught and sanctified, of His love for all.

—*Pope John XXIII*

PRAYER. *Lord Jesus, send the fire of Your love into my heart to purify it. Let that fire blaze, giving light to those lost in darkness and heat to those who suffer from the cold of loneliness.*

THE kingdom of this world has become the Kingdom of our Lord and of His Christ, and He will reign forever.

AUG.
30

—Rev 11:15

REFLECTION. God has handed over to us His own designs so that we may put them into operation, with complete freedom.

We are to assume full moral responsibility and demand of ourselves, where necessary, toil and sacrifice after the example of Christ.

—*Pope Pius XII*

PRAYER. *You have entrusted into my hands a tremendous task, O Lord. Let me respond with a mature and generous commitment to build up Your Kingdom upon this earth.*

I WILL set out and return to my Father and say to Him, "Father, I have sinned against heaven and against You."

AUG.
31

—Lk 15:18

REFLECTION. No matter where we look, no matter how we strive, if we wander far from God, we will not enjoy nature's tranquility, nor harmony and peace of soul.

We will be restless and harassed, as though tossed by fever.

—*Pope Pius XII*

PRAYER. *Lord God, as St. Augustine said, "We are restless until we rest in You." Let me rest in You, heart, soul, and strength.*

HO can ascend the mountain of
the Lord? or who can stand in His
holy place? The one whose hands
are sinless. —Ps 24:3-4

REFLECTION. Be witnesses to the love of the
Eucharistic Christ, a love that spurs us on to
unlimited generosity.

It also spurs us on to total surrender to
Him, and through Him to all those who seek
Him with a true heart.

—*Pope John Paul II*

PRAYER. *Lord Jesus, the Sacrament of the Eucharist is the Sacrament of Your unlimited
love. May I open my heart to that love and
share it with others.*

 ROM Him you are in Christ Jesus, Who
has become for us God-given wisdom
and justice and sanctification.
—1 Cor 1:30

REFLECTION. What a wonderful thing it is
when families realize the power they have.

This power works for the sanctification of
the world, the mutual sanctification of husband and wife, and the reciprocal influence
between parents and children.

—*Pope John Paul I*

PRAYER. *O Lord, let my family give witness to
Your Presence in our lives. May all be able to
say that truly, Christ dwells in my home.*

WHICH of you loves life and desires to see good days? Keep your tongues from evil.

SEPT.

3

—Ps 34:13-14

REFLECTION.   Let us at long last place human life itself among those precious assets that deserve our every protection.

Doctors and social workers, lawmakers, journalists, and teachers ought to be in conscience bound to call publicly for the legal protection of human life.   —*Pope John Paul II*

PRAYER. *Let me never think of life as inconvenient, O Lord, for it is Your most precious gift. May I protect it and celebrate it in myself and in others.*

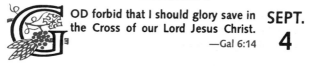**G**OD forbid that I should glory save in the Cross of our Lord Jesus Christ.

SEPT.

4

—Gal 6:14

REFLECTION.   The Cross of Christ! It is the last word of Divine Wisdom.

It is the ultimate source of Divine Power over human history.

—*Pope John Paul II*

PRAYER. *I adore You, O Christ, and I bless You, because by Your holy Cross You have redeemed the world.*

F old You laid the foundations of the earth, and the heavens are the work of Your hands. They will perish, but You remain. —Ps 102:26-27

REFLECTION. Observe the panorama of the firmament and the world; measure, if you can, their vastness. Affirm the incredible distinction between the Creator and the created world.

At the same time, recognize, confess, and celebrate the unshakable necessity that unites creation with its Creator. —Pope Paul VI

PRAYER. *O Lord, help me never to look at creation without seeing Your handiwork. Let me never allow anything created to prevent me from worshiping You, its Creator.*

 RAY for each other, that you may be saved. For the unceasing prayer of the just is powerful and effective. —Jas 5:16

REFLECTION. Pray, pray, pray; prayer is the key to the treasures of God.

It is the weapon of combat and of victory in every battle for good over evil.

—Pope Pius XII

PRAYER. *Heavenly Lord, let me never forget the power of prayer. Impress on my mind that the most important thing I can do for others and myself is to pray.*

VERYONE who hears My words and does not act upon them will be likened to a foolish person who built a house on sand.

SEPT. 7

—Mt 7:26

REFLECTION. There is one truth that we think is self-evident for all to see.

When the sacred rights of God and religion are ignored or infringed upon, the foundations of human society will sooner or later crumble and give way.

—Pope John XXIII

PRAYER. *O Lord, grant me the courage to profess my Faith, especially when it is inconvenient. Imbue in me the courage of those Saints who died for their Faith.*

 OD has given help to Israel His servant, mindful of His mercy—even as He spoke to our fathers.

SEPT. 8

—Lk 1:54-55

REFLECTION. Mary, accepting the will of the Father, opens the path of salvation and makes it possible—through the presence of the Kingdom of God—for His will to be done on earth as it is in heaven.

Mary, proclaiming the faithfulness of God for all generations, assures the victory of the poor and the lowly. —Pope John Paul II

PRAYER. *Dear Jesus, today we celebrate the feast of the Birth of Your Mother Mary. Help me to imitate her so that my soul will glorify the Lord and my spirit will rejoice in God my Savior.*

132

LOVE is not rude, is not self-seeking, is not easily angered, it keeps no record of wrongs.

—1 Cor 13:5

REFLECTION. Love is characterized by a deep respect for all people, regardless of their race, belief, or whatever makes them different from ourselves.

Love responds generously to the needs of the poor, and it is marked by compassion for those in sorrow. —*Pope John Paul II*

PRAYER. *O Lord, St. Peter Claver reached out in a truly heroic manner to those who were of a different race and religion from him. May my love be as fruitful and as color blind.*

———————————

WE who ... reflect the Lord's glory are being transformed into His very image with ever-increasing glory.

—2 Cor 3:18

REFLECTION. Christ is our Savior; He is the head of our immense body that is maturing: believing and redeemed humanity: the Church. It is He Who pardons us and enables us to do things greater than ourselves.

He is the defender of the poor and the consoler of the suffering. —*Pope Paul VI*

PRAYER. *Come, Lord Jesus. Come into our hearts, come into our world, and transform us into Your Kingdom. Let my heart be open to that transformation.*

ITH the heart a person believes unto justice, and with the mouth profession of faith is made unto salvation. **SEPT. 11**

—Rom 10:10

REFLECTION. Faith humiliates our pride of imagined self-sufficiency and at the same time opens our hearts to the immense and exalting proportions of the revealing Word of God.

On the threshold of the crib, of the Gospel, of salvation stands faith. —*Pope Paul VI*

PRAYER. *I need You, O Lord, and the love that You offer me. Let me believe and experience the most profound truth of salvation: that You love me.*

OME, children, hear me. I will teach you the fear of the Lord. **SEPT. 12**

—Ps 34:12

REFLECTION. The family must be a great school of piety, spirituality, and religious fidelity.

The Church has great trust in the delicate, authoritative, and irreplaceable religious teaching supplied by parents.

—*Pope Paul VI*

PRAYER. *O Lord, may my family find ways to express its faith. Teach its members to pray together, to talk to each other about our Faith, and to find a place in our lives for You.*

ING to the Lord a new song of praise in the assembly of His faithful ones.

SEPT. 13

—Ps 149:1

REFLECTION. Insist that your priests and those who collaborate with them in the liturgical service make ever more and more progress.

Let them enhance the dignity of the celebration, the quality of the readings, and the beauty of the singing. —*Pope John Paul II*

PRAYER. *O Lord, help me to realize that the Liturgy is a precious gift You have entrusted to Your Church. May I always participate in the Liturgy in a dignified manner, so that I may recognize Your Presence therein.*

 OR the doctrine of the Cross is foolishness to those who are perishing, but to those who are saved, that is, to us, it is the power of God.

SEPT. 14

—1 Cor 1:18

REFLECTION. On this day when Catholics around the world celebrate the Triumph of the Cross, the Church invites us to look once again at the meaning of Christian discipleship.

She invites us to understand the sacrifices it involves and place all our hope in our Crucified and Risen Savior. —*Pope John Paul II*

PRAYER. *O Lord, grant me the courage to take up my cross and follow You. Make me understand that it is through the Cross that I learn how to die with You, so that I may also rise with You.*

BLESSED is she who has believed, because the things the Lord has promised her will be accomplished.

SEPT. **15**

—Lk 1:45

REFLECTION. Mary not only leads us to the Mystery of the Cross like a teacher; she also participates in that Mystery. She suffers with Jesus and suffers with us.

With Jesus she also confronts and defeats the powers of evil. —*Pope John Paul II*

PRAYER. *O Lord, ease the pain of those who have lost children to drugs or violence. Console those whose children are rebelling and ungrateful. May they learn from Mary's trust, and share in her gentle love.*

LOVE bears with all things, believes all things, hopes all things, endures all things.

SEPT. **16**

—1 Cor 13:7

REFLECTION. Have no enemies. Conquer hostility with the power of love. Cultivate a mentality and practice of nonviolence.

Be open to the needy, the poor, the marginalized. May they be the specially invited guests at the table of your lives.

—*Pope John Paul II*

PRAYER. *O Lord, let me reach out to that one person in my life whom I would love to hate. If I cannot talk to that person, may I at least pray for that person until our relationship is healed.*

PUT on the new self who has been created according to God in justice and holiness of truth.

SEPT.

17

—Eph 4:24

REFLECTION. The first requirement for a constant listening to Christ is the full knowledge of yourselves.

A methodical and intelligent work on your personal life will open you to the perceptive and joyful formation of the new self.

—*Pope John Paul II*

PRAYER. *O Lord, teach me to be honest with myself. Help me to recognize my strengths as well as my weaknesses, and to allow You to transform both of these in Your love.*

WISDOM cries aloud in the street, in the open squares she raises her voice. She calls out down the crowded ways.

SEPT.

18

—Prov 1:20

REFLECTION. The voice of the Church is like the voice of a mother: it may seem monotonous at times.

However, it has a tone of tenderness and of strength that keeps us from evil and saves us.

—*Pope John XXIII*

PRAYER. *O Lord, You have given us Your Church to help us on our earthly pilgrimage and lead us to you. Protect her and guide her. Protect Pope N. and Bishop N. Guide them in Your Spirit.*

ESUS came and announced the good tidings of peace to you who were far off and of peace to those who were near.

—Eph 2:17

REFLECTION. Humankind has more than the right to peace.

It has also the right that all should pledge themselves to get rid of the causes that foment conflicts within a nation and between nations.

—*Pope Paul VI*

PRAYER. *I commit myself today, O Lord, to making this a better world, a place where all prejudice and all hatred disappear and Your love reigns.*

———————

HATEVER you do in word or in work, do all in the Name of the Lord Jesus, giving thanks to God the Father through Him. —Col 3:17

REFLECTION. We must have our own deep, continual inward life of prayer, of faith, of charity.

Without that we cannot participate usefully and wisely in the rebirth and reflowering of the liturgy. We cannot think, breathe, act, suffer, and fully hope with the living pilgrim Church. We must pray. —*Pope Paul VI*

PRAYER. *O Lord, teach me how to pray. Enable me to lift up to You the ordinary events of my day, so that what I say and do may be filled with Your love.*

LL Scripture is inspired by God and useful ... for training in holiness, so that all who belong to God may be equipped for every good work. —2 Tim 3:16

REFLECTION. The Incarnate Word of God continues to speak to the Church through the sacred books.

In reading and studying the Scriptures, Christians seek to know God and to understand God's plan for the human family.

—*Pope John Paul II*

PRAYER. *Lord Jesus, I commit myself to studying the Word of God, especially the Holy Gospels. Send Your Spirit into my heart so that I may understand what I read.*

E said to me, "My grace is sufficient for you, for strength is made perfect in weakness." —2 Cor 12:9

REFLECTION. If today we are living in a climate of public freedom and personal responsibility, we will have an increased duty to exercise our own critical moral judgment with vigilant assiduousness.

Temptations are very widespread and aggressive in our day. —*Pope John Paul II*

PRAYER. *O Lord, give me the courage to choose the good and to resist temptation. May my conduct never be a source of temptation to others.*

OD brought us to life together with Christ ... and seated us together in heaven in Christ.

SEPT. 23

—Eph 2:5-6

REFLECTION. Every burden is light when we are united to Christ, when it is He Who gives us the strength and breath to go on walking.

On the other hand, how heavy the burden is when it is carried without Christ!

—*Pope John Paul II*

PRAYER. *O Lord, let me never try to carry my burden alone because of a false pride. Teach me to trust completely in Your help and to reach out each day to my brothers and sisters as well.*

 Y sacrifice, O God, is a contrite spirit. You will not spurn a contrite and humble heart.

SEPT. 24

—Ps 51:19

REFLECTION. We need a docile heart in order to build an exemplary Christian community.

We need a spirit that is strong in the Faith in order to proclaim the love of God that conquers sin and saves in Christ Who died and is risen.

—*Pope John Paul II*

PRAYER. *Help me, O Lord, to find the balance between that gentle love that we always need and that tough love that is so difficult but that is necessary at times. Let the measure of my love not be what makes me feel good, but rather what the other needs.*

W E set our hearts at rest. Because if our heart blames us, God is greater than our heart.

—1 Jn 3:20

REFLECTION. Let Jesus Himself be the One to define your existence and direct your choices.

In this way the relationships among you may correspond always to the model of love given by the Heart of Christ, without either lapses or evasions. —*Pope John Paul II*

PRAYER. *Lord Jesus, help me to love as You have loved. May my love know no limits owing to fear or prejudice. Let my love bring me to Your Cross, and let Your Cross be mine.*

B Y this will all people know that you are My disciples, if you have love for one another.

—Jn 13:35

REFLECTION. At the heart of the human family and of the Church the work of assistance to the poor, the sick, the elderly, the disabled, the marginalized, the alienated, is as fruitful as the love that inspires it.

It is a living force of Christ's disciples that causes today's observers to repeat, "See how they love one another." —*Pope John Paul II*

PRAYER. *O Lord, is there a brother or sister about whom I have said, "Am I his or her keeper?" Let me today reach out and take the responsibility to make that person a part of my life.*

141

FOR I was a stranger, and you did not take Me in ...; sick and in prison, and you did not come to visit Me.

SEPT.
27

—Mt 25:43

REFLECTION.   Christ taught us not only how to suffer but also to help those who suffer.

And to encourage our generosity, He identified Himself with the person who suffers.

—*Pope John Paul II*

PRAYER. *Teach me compassion, O Lord. Make me like St. Vincent de Paul, who reached out to those most in need. Above all, let me remember what he always taught, that the poor owe us nothing when we help them, for the opportunity to help them is already our reward.*

———————

BUT I say to you, love your enemies, do good to those who hate you, and pray for those who persecute and calumniate you.

SEPT.
28

—Mt 5:44

REFLECTION.   There is nothing passive about nonviolence when it is chosen out of love. It has nothing to do with indifference.

It has everything to do with actively seeking to resist evil and conquer it with good.

—*Pope John Paul II*

PRAYER. *O Lord, may I respond to evil with good, to hate with love, to hurt given with an offer to heal, and to death with the sure hope of life.*

HE Angel [Gabriel] answered and said to her, "The Holy Spirit will come upon you ...; for nothing is impossible to God." —Lk 1:35-37

REFLECTION. Above all, one must never lose confidence in what the Spirit of God can accomplish in our own day. For as the Angel Gabriel said to the Virgin Mary, "Nothing is impossible to God."

Let our hearts be alive in faith and always steadfast in hope. —*Pope John Paul II*

PRAYER. *Almighty God, may the Archangels Michael, Gabriel, and Raphael teach me to trust in Your power and goodness. May I, too, sing of the Glory of the Lord.*

 OD'S Word is living and active and keener than any two-edged sword ... and a discerner of the thoughts and intentions. —Heb 4:12

REFLECTION. St. Jerome was the model of devotion and service to the revealed Word.

He never tired of reminding the Church that God Himself spoke to the soul of the sacred writers: "To be ignorant of the Scriptures is not to know Christ." —*Pope John Paul II*

PRAYER. *Lord Jesus, let me imitate St. Jerome and aspire to a deep and penetrating knowledge of Scripture. May I be ever more deeply nourished by the Divine Word and find in it a source of life.*

LORD, I am Your servant; I am Your servant, the child of Your handmaid; You have loosed my chains.

—Ps 116:16

REFLECTION. In order that your life may retain a taste of the feast, be dynamic and joyful in the service of others.

Seek to carry out what Christ asks of you; answer with Mary's "fiat": "I am the servant of the Lord" (Lk 1:38). —*Pope John Paul II*

PRAYER. *O Lord, let me always realize that doing good deeds carries its own reward, for it is the opportunity for me to grow in Your love. May this thought fill me ever with gratitude and joy.*

EE that you do not despise one of these little ones. For I tell you, their Angels in heaven always behold the face of My Father in heaven.

—Mt 18:10

REFLECTION. Holiness is the awareness of being "watched over," watched over by God. Saints know very well their frailty, the precariousness of their existence.

Yet they are not frightened. They feel secure in spite of all this. —*Pope John Paul II*

PRAYER. *Lord Jesus, You have promised that You would have our Angels watch over us. Let my Angel always be close at hand to protect and guide, intercede and respond in Your Name.*

ECAUSE you are sons, God has sent the Spirit of His Son into our hearts, crying, "Abba, Father."

—Gal 4:6

REFLECTION. Arriving at a deeper awareness of Christ demands also a deeper awareness of the Holy Spirit.

"To know Who Christ is" and "to know Who the Spirit is" are two indissolubly linked requirements, the one implying the other.

—*Pope John Paul II*

PRAYER. *Come, Holy Spirit, inspire my prayers. Beloved Guest of my soul, help me to pray well. Give breath to me as I pray in, with, and through Christ.*

 M Y trust is in You, O Lord. I say, "You are my God." My destiny is in Your hands.

OCT.
4

—Ps 31:15-16

REFLECTION. In the spirit of St. Francis of Assisi, I urge you all to open your hearts to God's love, to respond by your prayers and by the deeds of your lives.

Let go of your doubts and fears, and allow the mercy of God to draw you to His Heart.

—*Pope John Paul II*

PRAYER. *O Lord, let me always trust in You. May my prayer always be that of St. Francis, "My God and my All; my God and my All; my God and my All."*

DO not be a witness against your neighbor without just cause, thus committing folly with your lips.

**OCT.
5**

—Prov 24:28

REFLECTION. Whenever you refuse to accuse someone without proof, you announce the coming of the Kingdom of God and His justice.

From that Kingdom no one is excluded.

—*Pope John Paul II*

PRAYER. *O Lord, help me to realize the power of my words, how gossip and exaggeration concerning another can do so much damage. Let my words be just and charitable, always building up and not tearing down.*

I HAVE swept away your offenses like a cloud, your sins like a mist. Return to Me, for I have redeemed you.

**OCT.
6**

—Is 44:22

REFLECTION. To conserve and increase that Divine life in which you share, strive for a continuous conversion of mind and heart, firmly struggling with sin that destroys the life of your soul.

Return with confidence to God our Father with the repentance that flows from love of Him Who is Supreme Goodness. —*Pope John Paul II*

PRAYER. *Heavenly Lord, I have turned from Your love in sin. Help me to return to You. Take me once again in Your arms and hold me and never let me go.*

T HE Mother of Jesus said to Him, "They have no wine." ... His Mother said to the waiters, "Do whatever He tells you." —Jn 2:3-5

REFLECTION. I want to recommend the Rosary to you in a special way. It is a source of profound Christian life. Try to pray it every day alone or with your family.

Meditate on those scenes of the life of Jesus and Mary of which the Joyful, Sorrowful, and Glorious Mysteries remind us. —*Pope John Paul II*

PRAYER. *Lord Jesus, today is the feast of our Lady of the Rosary. May the prayers of Your Holy Mother for the world lead me to pray the Rosary more often and with greater fervor.*

Y OU are built upon the foundation of the Apostles and Prophets with Christ Jesus Himself as the chief cornerstone. —Eph 2:20

REFLECTION. Change must be judged not so much for its own sake as for its content, its finality.

Is the new of today leading us to a really better Christianity?

—*Pope Paul VI*

PRAYER. *O Lord, grant me insight into the choices that I make, whether they be life choices or everyday decisions. Let them all be grounded in You so that they may all build up Your Kingdom.*

THIS grace was given to me ... to enlighten all people as to what is the dispensation of the Mystery that was hidden in God. —Eph 3:8-9

REFLECTION. A deeply Christian life cannot be sustained by religious feelings alone or by a vague identification with a religious tradition.

What is required is an ever greater understanding of the Mystery of Salvation that is revealed in Christ and handed down in Sacred Scripture and Church teaching. —*Pope John Paul II*

PRAYER. *O Lord, I commit myself to study my Faith ever more, to read Scripture regularly, and to be familiar with the teaching of the Church regarding the Mystery of Salvation.*

BUT the Advocate, the Holy Spirit, ... will teach you all things and bring to mind everything I have said to you. —Jn 14:26

OCT. 10

REFLECTION. In the past the attacks against the Christian Faith came from without, from forces contrary and extraneous to the believing community.

Today the snares arise from within, in the context of the rapid social change that is taking place in our age. —*Pope John Paul II*

PRAYER. *O Lord, let me be ready to defend the Church, acknowledging her human weaknesses. At the same time, help me to recognize that the Holy Spirit is guiding her even today.*

YOU are the light of the world. A city set on a mountain cannot be hidden.

—Mt 5:14

REFLECTION. We have a responsibility regarding the light that has been passed to us. We cannot enclose it within the four walls of our "I."

We must also communicate it to others. We must shine with it it before all.

—*Pope John Paul II*

PRAYER. *May I be like the glass in a stained glass window, O Lord, allowing Your light to shine through, while at the same time coloring it with my own talents and gifts.*

———————

FOR through the Law I have died to the Law. With Christ I am nailed to the Cross.

—Gal 2:19

REFLECTION. Certainly, you are not unaware of how much the path of love can cost.

Christ Himself reminds you of it from atop the Cross.

—*Pope John Paul II*

PRAYER. *Lord Jesus, You asked us to take up our crosses and follow You. Strengthen me to embrace my cross. Grant me the love to carry it willingly and the hope to be filled with Your joy.*

M Y mouth shall meditate truth, but my lips abhor wickedness. All the words of my mouth are sincere.

OCT.
13

—Prov 8:7-8

REFLECTION. Hold truth in holy respect; fear to offend it, to betray it. Impose upon yourself the discipline of silence, of moderation, of patience.

Truth seeks only to be proclaimed in its entirety.

—Pope John XXIII

PRAYER. *O Lord, help me to run from half-truths and convenient lies. Let me never debase the truth with falsehood. May I be known as a person of my word.*

A S the sufferings of Christ abound in us, so also through Christ does our consolation abound.

OCT.
14

—2 Cor 1:5

REFLECTION. Those who see suffering with merely human eyes cannot understand its meaning.

We Christians know that suffering can be converted if we offer it to God. It can become an instrument of salvation, a path to holiness, that helps us to reach heaven. —*Pope John Paul II*

PRAYER. *Father, You called Your Son to the Cross, for You knew that the Cross was great love. May I see my own crosses as opportunities to learn and share that same love.*

EACE I leave with you, My peace I give to you; not as the world gives do I give to you. Do not let your heart be troubled.
—Jn 14:27

REFLECTION. The presence of contemplatives in the midst of God's people fulfills the same function as the heart in the human body.

As the heart, though hidden, is the source of all the body's activities, so contemplation, though hidden, gives life and holiness to the Church. —*Pope John Paul II*

PRAYER. *O Lord, let me never value things as the world sees them. Help me to value them according to a spiritual criterion, which sees great value in silence and prayer, value that can change the world.*

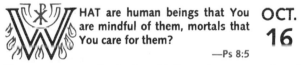

HAT are human beings that You are mindful of them, mortals that You care for them?
—Ps 8:5

REFLECTION. God the Father loves each of you. It is not that He loves you too, but that He loves you most of all.

His is a love so strong that it melts the hardness of the human heart. His is a justice that is clothed in mercy. —*Pope John Paul II*

PRAYER. *Thank You, Father, for a parent's love that knows no limits. Thank You, for cherishing me, Your child, as precious in Your eyes.*

151

NOW I exhort the presbyters among you, ... tend the flock of God that is among you, governing willingly according to God. —1 Pt 5:1

REFLECTION. In order to continue and grow the Gospel life-style as the early Christians did, you must be united among yourselves and with your bishops.

You must persevere in the liturgical and sacramental life and meditate on the truth of the Faith within your heart. —*Pope John Paul II*

PRAYER. *O Lord, St. Ignatius of Antioch cared for his flock and bore witness to the Faith. May our bishop N. hold firm to the Faith with courage and lead his flock with gentleness.*

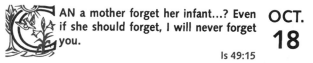

CAN a mother forget her infant...? Even if she should forget, I will never forget you.

Is 49:15

REFLECTION. God's love is tender and merciful, patient and full of understanding.

In the Scriptures, and also in the living memory of the Church, the love of God is indeed depicted and has been experienced as the compassionate love of a mother.

—*Pope John Paul II*

PRAYER. *O Lord, the Prophet told us that even if a mother were to forget her child, You would never forget us. May I ever experience that maternal love with which You love Your beloved children.*

AND bearing the Cross for Himself, He went forth to the place called the Skull, ... where they crucified Him.
—Jn 19:17-18

REFLECTION. The Cross was not an accident in the journey made by Jesus.

It was an element consciously willed for the redemption of humankind.

—*Pope John Paul II*

PRAYER. *Lord Jesus, You willed to die on the Cross for our redemption. Help me to believe with all my heart that Your victorious Cross is the only hope of humankind. Let it lead me to the joy and peace of the Resurrection and eternal life.*

I HAVE proclaimed Your justice in the vast assembly.... I have made no secret of Your love and Your truth.
—Ps 40:10-11

REFLECTION. It is not enough merely to formulate a social doctrine. It must be translated into reality.

This is particularly true of the Church's social doctrine, which has truth as its light, justice as its objective, and love as its driving force.

—*Pope John XXIII*

PRAYER. *O Lord, may I always seek Your truth, fight for justice for all, and love the world into healing.*

PERFORM your work at the proper time, and in His own time God will give you your reward.

—Sir 51:30

REFLECTION. Choosing a carpenter for His "foster father" and becoming a carpenter Himself, Christ has enriched human work with a dignity that cannot be equaled.

Now all who work know that they are doing something Divine, which can even be linked with God's initial work. —*Pope John Paul II*

PRAYER. *Almighty God, enable me to see my work as a participation in Your work of creation. Let me marvel in my dignity of being a cocreator of Your Kingdom.*

OW for yourselves justice, reap the fruit of piety,... for it is time to seek the Lord till He comes and rains down justice.

—Hos 10:12

REFLECTION. As far as the Christian is concerned, ethical behavior in public life must be restored.

However, this must go hand in hand with an awareness of one's identity and of the message of salvation of which one is the humble but diligent witness. —*Pope John Paul II*

PRAYER. *Lord Jesus, move the hearts of those who lead our country. May Your Spirit guide them to give witness to Your love and to defend the rights of their citizens, especially those who are too weak to defend themselves.*

TURN to me and have mercy on me, for I am poor and needy.

—Ps 25:16

REFLECTION. In prayer, we come to see the stark reality of our own poverty, the absolute need we have for a Savior.

We discover in a more profound degree the many ways in which we ourselves are poor and needy, and thus we begin to feel an increasing solidarity with all the poor.

—*Pope John Paul II*

PRAYER. *O Lord, let me always recognize that what I do for the poor should be based upon the solidarity I feel with them. We are both dependent upon You for all we have.*

RECEIVE My instruction in preference to silver and knowledge instead of choice gold.

—Prov 8:10

REFLECTION. There is a theological truth behind the depictions of Mary most holy with the Infant Jesus in her arms.

She gives you Jesus and leads you toward Jesus in the Eucharist, the center of your personal life and community; to Jesus, the Word of life. —*Pope John Paul II*

PRAYER. *Lead me, Mary, to your Son. May I follow your example and make Him present again in a world that needs His love.*

TODAY, salvation has come to this house.... For the Son of Man came to seek and to save what was lost.

OCT.
25

—Lk 19:10

REFLECTION. We can all get lost at times, lost within ourselves or lost in the world about us.

Allow Christ to find you, to speak to you, to ask of you whatever He wants.

—*Pope John Paul II*

PRAYER. *I have allowed myself to get lost, Lord Jesus, and I need You. Show me what You want me to do. For You are my way, my truth, and my very life.*

NOW the Lord permitted this trial to happen to him, so as to give an example of his patience to others.

OCT.
26

—Tob 2:12

REFLECTION. Feelings that motivate people reveal their profound stability during difficult moments.

It is then that mutual surrender and love take root in their hearts, because true love does not think of itself but of how it can promote the true good of the loved one.

—*Pope John Paul II*

PRAYER. *O Lord, help me to realize that the difficult moments in my life and my relationships with others are really opportunities for a greater love. Enable me to choose that love—for it is its own reward.*

ING praise to the Lord, all you His faithful ones, and give thanks to His holy Name.

—Ps 30:5

REFLECTION. Sing with your voices, sing with your hearts! Make people understand how beautiful it is to pray singing, as you do, with the Church and for the Church.

Spread joy, spread goodness, spread light.

—*Pope Paul VI*

PRAYER. *Let me raise up my voice to You, O Lord. May I sing Your praises for all the wonderful things You have done for the whole world and especially for me. Enable me to spread Your joy, goodness, and light to all those I meet.*

 OR if someone comes and preaches ... a different Gospel from the one you accepted, you submit to it easily enough.

—2 Cor 11:4

REFLECTION. We know that we have no riches other than that which we have received.

Therefore, we must dare to question those who are going astray or who are leading others astray on deadend streets of a closed individualism or of an indifference to essential values. —*Pope John Paul II*

PRAYER. *O Lord, give me the courage to use tough love when that is what my loved ones need. Help me to challenge them when I see they are involved in self-destructive behavior.*

HE love of Christ impels us because we know that ... Christ died for all so that those who are alive should no longer live for themselves. —2 Cor 5:14-15

REFLECTION. Only Christ's law, only Christ's grace can renew and restore private and public life.

He alone can redress the true balance of rights and duties, check unbridled self-interest, control passion, implement and perfect the course of justice with His overflowing charity. —Pope Pius XII

PRAYER. *Lord Jesus, let me never be selfish in my attitude toward society. May I be generous, seeking the good of the other rather than my own pleasure.*

E will walk in the Name of the Lord, our God, forever and ever. —Mic 4:5

REFLECTION. A new era is unfolding of faithfulness to the Holy Spirit, of love of the crucified Christ, of dedication to one's brothers and sisters, of the building up of a more human and just society.

We do not want to lag behind. Forward, in the Name of the Lord. —Pope Paul VI

PRAYER. *May my every action, every word be filled with love for You, O Lord. Help me to make You the focal point of my whole life.*

UT of the depths I cry to You, O Lord; Lord, hear my voice. Let Your ears be attentive to my cry for mercy. **OCT. 31**
—Ps 130:1-2

REFLECTION. The person who does not feel indebted to God remains entangled in restless inclination toward self.

But to the heart of the truly humble believer the Lord reveals His presence, His sovereignty in saving power, His justice in the infinite greatness of His mercy. —*Pope John Paul II*

PRAYER. *O Lord, I acknowledge my need of Your mercy. I am a sinner; I have done things that have shut me off from Your love and from my sisters and brothers. Forgive me; heal me; love me.*

HOW yourself in all things an example of good works. In your teaching show integrity, seriousness, and soundness of speech. **NOV. 1**
—Ti 2:7

REFLECTION. Christians need human examples in order to better follow God.

Let us not overlook this most effective means to holiness, that of following the example of those who preceded us.

—*Pope Paul VI*

PRAYER. *Martyrs and Apostles, pray for me. Missionaries and teachers, pray for me. Holy men and women, pray for me. All you Saints of God, pray for me.*

159

FOR if he had no hope that those who had fallen would rise again, it would have been superfluous and foolish to pray for the dead. —2 Mac 12:44

NOV. 2

REFLECTION. We have inherited from the most ancient Christian communities the following certainty.

There is an intense participation in life between us and the sisters and brothers who are in heavenly glory or who are still being purified after death. —*Pope John Paul II*

PRAYER. *O Lord, on this All Souls Day, I pray for all my departed family members, relatives, and benefactors. Eternal rest grant to them, and let perpetual light shine upon them.*

YOU are my rock and my fortress. For Your Name's sake, You will lead and guide me. —Ps 31:4

NOV. 3

REFLECTION. Brother Martin had three loves: Christ crucified, Our Lady of the Rosary, and St. Dominic.

He also had three passions: charity, especially toward the poor and the sick; a very vigorous penance that he regarded as "the price of love"; and nourishing those virtues, humility. —*Pope Paul VI*

PRAYER. *O Lord, may I learn from the example of St. Martin de Porres and develop a balanced spirituality. Let me not run away from those aspects of the spiritual life that I find difficult.*

160

SAY to you ... unless you repent, you will all perish in the same way.

—Lk 13:5

REFLECTION. To live the Christian life well there is need of continual repairing, of recurring reforms, of repeated renewals.

The Christian life is not soft or easy. It is not blindly optimistic. It is joyous but it is not happy-go-lucky.

—Pope Paul VI

PRAYER. O Lord, let me find a place for penitential practices in my life and in my spirituality. May I see fasting and mortification not as drudgery, but rather as avenues to freedom.

OD is able to make all grace abound in you, so that ... having all that you need, you will abound in every good work.

—2 Cor 9:8

REFLECTION. Grace is Divine Life in the human soul, fruit of reconciliation, gifts of God in Jesus.

It is the beginning of eternal life, that is, of salvation.

—Pope John Paul II

PRAYER. Pour Your grace upon me, O Lord; let it be like a river that nourishes the land. May it make my heart fruitful and my faith verdant and alive.

HEN you pray, go into your room, close the door, and pray to your Father in secret.

NOV. 6

—Mt 6:6

REFLECTION. We must nourish in ourselves a personal religious activity. To meditate. To pray.

To pray means to ascend; to ascend to the first source of everything: of being, thought, action, enjoyment.

—*Pope Paul VI*

PRAYER. *Lord Jesus, teach me how to pray even as You taught Your disciples. Send Your Spirit into my heart so that I may pray with You to the Father.*

ND there was a certain poor man named Lazarus, who lay at the rich man's gate,...longing to be filled with crumbs from his table.

NOV. 7

—Lk 16:19

REFLECTION. We ask you to go out to meet poor Lazarus, in his hunger and misery.

Make yourself his neighbor, so that he can recognize in your eyes the eyes of Christ welcoming him, and in your hands the hands of the Lord sharing His gifts.

—*Pope Paul VI*

PRAYER. *Lord Jesus, You repeatedly taught Your disciples that the poor are our brothers and sisters. Help me to find ways to reach out to them in my own life.*

FOR the wages of sin is death, but the gift of God is life everlasting in Christ Jesus our Lord.

NOV. 8

—Rom 6:23

REFLECTION. Death, understood as the complete and final annihilation of our being, does not exist, especially for us believers.

We already have our place in the Mystical Body of Christ, destined for resurrection and, God willing, eternal life. This is the truth!

—*Pope Paul VI*

PRAYER. *Lord Jesus, I believe that Your love is stronger than death, Your life more powerful than the grave. Let me always live in the radiance of that life-giving love.*

THE Lord has...sent me to bring glad tidings to the lowly, to heal the brokenhearted, and to proclaim liberty to the captives.

NOV. 9

—Is 61:1

REFLECTION. A Christian who is really Catholic must be an apostle: with prayer, with example, with oblation, with suffering, with activity, with discipline, with organization.

A widespread effort of faith is the duty of this hour for every member of the Mystical Body of Christ.

—*Pope Paul VI*

PRAYER. *O Lord, You called St. Peter from his fishing, St. Matthew from his tax collecting. Call me now to follow You and to proclaim the Good News to all whom I meet.*

163

I F anyone says to you, "Behold, here is the Christ," or "There He is," do not believe it.

—Mt 24:23

REFLECTION. The truth that Jesus has revealed remains throughout eternity, taught and defended by the Church, who has been appointed Mother and Teacher of Truth.

We must not let ourselves be disconcerted by events; we must always have a supernatural view of things and events. —*Pope John Paul II*

PRAYER. *O Lord, in these times when I often hear negative things about the Church, help me to remember all the good that the Church is accomplishing. Keep me from being discouraged, for You are the source of my hope.*

 VEN though I should walk in the midst of the shadow of death, I will fear no evil, for You are at my side.

—Ps 23:4

REFLECTION. Where others lose themselves, those who trust in Christ can do everything.

In harmony with order and the justification and magnificence of God, they rise above the disorders and storms of the world with equal courage and order. —*Pope Pius X*

PRAYER. *O Lord, You are my all. Guide me through the dark valleys of my life; lead me to Your verdant pasture.*

BE children of your Father in heaven, Who makes His sun to rise on the good and the evil, and sends rain on the just and the unjust. —Mt 5:45

REFLECTION. Only by becoming more faithful disciples of Jesus Christ can we hope to travel the path of unity under the guidance of the Holy Spirit.

Only by accepting Jesus as Lord of our lives can we empty ourselves of negative thinking about each other. —*Pope John Paul II*

PRAYER. *Lord Jesus, enable me to see others through Your eyes. The Father sends rain upon the good and the bad, for He loves everyone. Let me be filled with that same love.*

ON behalf of Christ, therefore, we are acting as ambassadors, God, as it were acting through us. —2 Cor 5:20

REFLECTION. Much to be envied are those who can give their lives for something greater than themselves in loving service to others.

This, more than words or deeds alone, is what draws people to Christ.

—*Pope John Paul II*

PRAYER. *O Lord, your servant St. Frances Cabrini spent her life serving the poor. May she be a model to me of service, and may I be as willing as she was to reach out to those at the margins of society.*

EATH is swallowed up in victory. O death, where is your victory? O death, where is your sting?

NOV.
14

—1 Cor 15:54-55

REFLECTION. Death can be an experience of extraordinary solidarity. Death makes us brothers and sisters.

In a world that casts death aside and does everything to hide it, it is urgently necessary to recall the inevitability of an event that is part of the history of every person. —*Pope John Paul II*

PRAYER. *Lord, in this month that we dedicate to remembering the dead, help me to meditate upon my own death. Let me do so not in a morbid fascination or fatalism, but rather in recognition that in death I come home to You.*

AITH then depends on hearing, and hearing on the Word of Christ.... "Their voice has gone forth into all the earth."

NOV.
15

—Rom 10:17-18

REFLECTION. The Faith that we have received as a gift is a sacred trust that must be handed on to others.

There is an urgency about the truths of Christianity, a missionary dimension to its saving message. —*Pope John Paul II*

PRAYER. *O Lord, help me to have the courage to share my Faith with just one person today. Let me not be ashamed, but rather filled with joy that I can share what is most precious to me.*

G OD sets the lonely in families; he leads forth prisoners to prosperity.
—Ps 68:7

REFLECTION. Genuine happiness of the home is based on love that gives itself and sacrifices itself simply and perseveringly.

This love can be sustained only with the food of faith, and faith is a gift of God that is nourished in prayer and the Sacraments.

—*Pope John Paul II*

PRAYER. *O Lord, may I always remember that no matter how good my intentions are, I cannot hope to love and build up my family as much as I would like to without Your grace.*

A LL of these people gave their gifts to God out of their wealth. But [this widow] out of her poverty gave all that she had to live on.
—Lk 21:4

REFLECTION. The laity, because of their vocation to be the salt of the earth and the light of the world, should be well grounded in the Church's social doctrine.

Then, through their presence in public life, they should contribute to strengthening the fabric of society.
—*Pope John Paul II*

PRAYER. *O Lord, St. Elizabeth of Hungary gave up her riches to serve the poor. May her example inspire me to take stock of my possessions and to be willing to share that which I do not really need.*

G O into the whole world and proclaim the Gospel to all creation. Whoever believes and is baptized will be saved. —Mk 16:15-16

NOV. 18

REFLECTION. In order to become apostles, as the Church wishes us all to be today, there is need of a deep love for Christ, a personal love, a true love, and a full love.

The apostolate is an overflowing of love, an outburst of love, turning into witness and action. —*Pope Paul VI*

PRAYER. *Almighty Lord, let me view my faith not as an obligation, but as a wondrous gift. May I be so filled with joy that I proclaim Christ's love to all.*

ET all bitterness and wrath and indignation and wrangling and reviling be removed from you, along with all malice. —Eph 4:31

NOV. 19

REFLECTION. Peace is needed. This refers to inner peace, peace of the conscience freed from all the fragmentation caused by sin and open to the true good.

It also means peace with others, in mutual respect and friendship, made of truth and love. —*Pope John Paul II*

PRAYER. *Lord, make me an instrument of Your peace. Where there is hatred, let me sow love. And where there is injury, let me sow pardon.*

O Him Who ... made us a Kingdom and priests to God His Father belong glory and dominion forever.

—Rev 1:6

NOV. 20

REFLECTION. It is in our power to correspond with continuing increase in grace that God wishes to grant us.

He does so to help us advance, without hesitation or stumbling, toward His Kingdom.

—*Pope John Paul II*

PRAYER. *O Lord, let my one goal in life be Your Kingdom, both here on earth and in the life to come. May I recognize that the only sure means to that goal is my cooperation with Your continual grace.*

LL who love me, I also love. And those who seek me find me.

—Prov 8:17

NOV. 21

REFLECTION. Before Jesus ever spoke about Himself and His mission, Mary spoke of Him to those who came to visit the Child.

And they were amazed to learn how much God had done for the salvation of Israel and the entire humanity. —*Pope John Paul II*

PRAYER. *Blessed Mother Mary, teach me about Your Son. Instruct me in His ways; protect me from those things that separate me from Him; and lead me home to Him in heaven with you forever.*

ALL of God's creations differ ..., yet none of them has He made in vain. For each is good. Can one ever see enough of their splendor? —Sir 42:25

NOV. 22

REFLECTION. You produce music, poetry and art, drama, painting and sculpture, and literature.

All those things reflect the soul of a nation being influenced by the Spirit of Christ for the perfection of humanity. —*Pope John Paul II*

PRAYER. *O Lord, teach me to celebrate that which is beautiful, for it gives witness to Your beauty. And let me promote cultural activities, for these can bring me closer to You.*

IF your enemies are hungry, give them food; if they are thirsty, give them drink. In so doing, you will heap coals of fire upon their heads. —Rom 12:20

NOV. 23

REFLECTION. To preach the Gospel of forgiveness seems absurd to human politics, because in the natural economy justice does not often permit forgiveness.

But in the Christian economy, it is not absurd. Difficult, yes, but not absurd.

—*Pope Paul VI*

PRAYER. *Teach me to forgive, Lord Jesus. Help me to realize that those who have hurt me are hurting persons themselves. Let me not aggravate their hurt and mine with bitterness and hate. Let me heal them and myself with love.*

FOR a whole year they ... taught a great multitude. And it was in Antioch that the disciples were first called "Christians."
—Acts 11:26

REFLECTION. The Church reminds us and admonishes us: Christians, be conscious of your state; Christians, be consistent; Christians, be faithful; Christians, be strong.

In a word, Christians, be Christians!

—*Pope Paul VI*

PRAYER. *O Lord, let "Christian" not only be a name I call myself, but my very identity. May I view Your call to the Christian Faith as the most precious thing You have given me and always strive to act as a Christian.*

 NOW the body is not for immorality but for the Lord, and the Lord for the body.
—1 Cor 6:13

REFLECTION. Every individual is a living expression of unity, and the human body is not just an instrument or item of property but shares in the individual's value as a human being.

It follows, therefore, that the body cannot be treated as something to be disposed of at will.
—*Pope John Paul II*

PRAYER. *O Lord, let me always treat my body as a gift from You. May I give up those things that harm the health of my body and do those things that promote its well-being.*

171

BEFORE I formed you in the womb I knew you, before you were born I set you apart and appointed you.

—Jer 1:5

REFLECTION. A vocation is a call that comes from God's sovereign power and free gift.

However, such a call must find an open path in the heart. It must enter into the depths of the subject's thoughts, feelings and will, in order to influence one's moral behavior.

—*Pope John Paul II*

PRAYER. *O Lord, I believe that You called me before I was born. Help me to discern where that call should lead me, and give me the courage to respond with my whole heart, my entire soul, and my very life.*

HE went up to him and bandaged his wounds, pouring on oil and wine.... He brought him to an inn and took care of him.

—Lk 10:34

REFLECTION. Be firm in rejecting injustice! Be strong in conceiving and accomplishing gestures of equity, humanity, and peace, gestures that will unravel the tangled skin of violence.

Humanity expects this service from you: it is your honor and your duty. —*Pope Paul VI*

PRAYER. *Lord Jesus, let me consider it an honor to love those who are unlovable. May I consider it a duty to heal their wounds.*

HOEVER has compassion on the poor lends to the Lord, Who will repay the good deed in full.

—Prov 19:17

REFLECTION. Such is the charity of the Christians convinced that their possessions have a social function.

For they believe that to use what is superfluous to their needs in favor of one who does not have the necessities is not an optional act of generosity but a duty. *—Pope John XXIII*

PRAYER. *O Lord, may I always think of my possessions as things with which You have entrusted to me for my good, but especially for the good of those who are poor.*

HERE is no fear in love. Indeed perfect love casts out fear, because fear brings punishment.

—1 Jn 4:18

REFLECTION. All of us who have faith in our Lord Jesus Christ know that our death will not be totally different from the rest of our earthly journey.

It too will be God's love coming upon us, but God's love in its transforming fullness.

—Pope John Paul II

PRAYER. *O Lord, the First Letter of John speaks of love overcoming fear. May my love be so pure and strong that I am able to see death for what it is, a transformation into a greater love.*

ROOTED and grounded in love, may you be able ... to know Christ's love, which surpasses understanding.

NOV.
30

—Eph 3:19

REFLECTION. Just as the Apostles gathered in the Upper Room, so we today share the Bread of everlasting life, as we join our praise to that of the faithful of the whole world.

We pause in amazement, in silent adoration, before the great Mystery of our Faith.

—*Pope John Paul II*

PRAYER. *O Bread of Life; O Mystery of Love; O Holy Banquet. May I love You, Jesus, with even a fraction of the enormous love You show me in this Blessed Sacrament.*

YOUR mother was like a vine planted by the water, fruitful and full of branches because of abundant water.

DEC.
1

—Ez 19:10

REFLECTION. The Church is our Mother: a Mother who nourishes and reconciles.

We cannot criticize our Mother as if she were a stranger, for we love the person who gave us life.

—*Pope John Paul II*

PRAYER. *Lord Jesus, may I always love Your Church with a familial love. Teach me to be grateful for all the good and love she has brought me.*

174

WHO has shown you how to flee from the wrath to come? Bring forth fruit befitting repentance.

DEC. 2

—Mt 3:7-8

REFLECTION. Our evangelizing zeal must spring from true holiness of life.

In addition, as the Second Vatican Council suggests, preaching must in its turn make the preacher grow in holiness, which is nourished by prayer and by love for the Eucharist.

—*Pope Paul VI*

PRAYER. *O Lord, let me never ask why "they" do not convert, but rather "how" I must convert. Enable me to recognize that my conversion is a powerful invitation to others to seek conversion.*

FOR He Who avenges blood has remembered. He has not forgotten the cry of the poor.

DEC. 3

—Ps 9:13

REFLECTION. The call to prayer must precede the call to action, but the call to action must truly accompany the call to prayer.

In prayer we discover the needs of our brothers and sisters and make them our own, because in prayer we discover that their needs are the needs of Christ. —*Pope John Paul II*

PRAYER. *Lord Jesus, let me find a quiet place where I may pray and gain perspective. Help me to use this prayer time to learn Your ways, and, like You, to hear the cry of the poor.*

175

AFTER hearing the Word of God, they hold it fast with a right and good heart and bear fruit in patience.

DEC. 4

—Lk 8:15

REFLECTION. At this point, the drama is either "Yes" or "No" for the modern generation that has shown that it has understood the possibility and happiness of an encounter with Christ.

Christ is speaking from His crib, "Blest are they who hear the Word of God and keep it" (Lk 11:28). —*Pope Paul VI*

PRAYER. *Lord Jesus, let this Advent be a season in which I learn to say "Yes" to You and Your call. Teach me to say "No" to everything that would keep me away from You.*

HOLY, holy, holy is the Lord of hosts!... All the earth is full of His glory.

DEC. 5

—Is 6:3

REFLECTION. Humility reduces the vision one has of oneself down to its proper proportion in accordance with right reason.

The gift of fear of God follows close upon it to perfect the soul by making the Christian aware that God alone is the highest good.

—*Pope John XXIII*

PRAYER. *Help me to recognize and accept my limitations, O Lord. Let me know that You are my Creator, all Holy, all Loving, and I am Your creation, who depend upon You for every breath I take.*

WHAT is lacking to the sufferings of Christ I fill up in my flesh for His Body, which is the Church.

—Col 1:24

REFLECTION. Over the centuries shining pages have been written of heroism in suffering accepted and offered in union with Christ.

Likewise we see humble service to the poor and the sick, in whose tormented flesh the presence of the poor, crucified Christ has been recognized. —*Pope John Paul II*

PRAYER. *Lord Jesus, I often wonder whether I do enough as a response to my faith. Teach me what You would have me do. Give me the opportunity to grow in Your love.*

OPENING His mouth, He taught them, saying, "Blessed are the poor in spirit, for theirs is the Kingdom of heaven...."

—Mt 5:2-3

REFLECTION. The Beatitudes demand a spiritual renewal based on the radical following of Christ the Priest, Teacher, and Good Shepherd.

This means making a gift of one's life, an offering to God Who calls us to build the spiritual edifice that is the Church.

—*Pope John Paul II*

PRAYER. *O Lord, teach me how to be poor in spirit, merciful, a peacemaker. Let the message of the Beatitudes transform me, so that I may follow You with heart, soul, and strength.*

HAIL, full of grace; the Lord is with you. Blessed are you among women.

DEC.
8

—Lk 1:28

REFLECTION. Mary Immaculate, she who has been redeemed in a privileged manner, is the sign of the beginning of God"s project to make all things new.

It is she who unveils, with her singular grace, the new life introduced by God the Father into the most intimate depths of the human person. —*Pope John Paul II*

PRAYER. *Mary, conceived without sin, pray for us who have recourse to you. Pray especially for the enemies of the Church and those most in need of your mercy.*

PETER fell down at Jesus' knees, saying, "Depart from me for I am a sinful man, O Lord."

DEC.
9

—Lk 5:8

REFLECTION. In Advent, the Church arouses in us the consciousness of our sins.

She also urges us, by restraining our desires and practicing voluntary mortification of the body, to recollect ourselves in meditation and experience a longing desire to return to God. —*Pope Pius XII*

PRAYER. *O Lord, I am a sinner. I do not deserve that You come under my roof. Heal me, forgive me, so that I can fully welcome Your birth on Christmas Day.*

THEY returned to their own town of Nazareth. And the Child grew and became strong. He was full of wisdom and the grace of God. —Lk 2:39-40

DEC.
10

REFLECTION. Nazareth is the school in which one can begin to understand the life of Jesus: the school of the Gospel.

Here one learns to watch, to listen, to meditate, and to penetrate the most profound and mysterious meaning of this manifestation of the Son of God. —*Pope John XXIII*

PRAYER. *Lord Jesus, let me meditate upon how Mary and Joseph spoke to You of God's love, how You learned to work, and how You learned to surrender Your life in love.*

 RECEIVE the Word, which has been planted in you and can save you. But be doers of the Word, and not hearers only. —Jas 1:21-22

DEC.
11

REFLECTION. All of us are capable of expressing ourselves, of transmitting our message to the world. But at the same time, each one of us must be a hearer.

Our message will be more fitting the more the hearing of the Word of God is already present in our message. —*Pope John Paul II*

PRAYER. *Teach me to listen, O Lord. Let me hear the call of the Prophets, the voice of the Baptist, and the wonder of all creation at the fact that the Creator has become a creature.*

HAVE heard your prayer, and I have chosen this place for myself as a house of sacrifice.
—2 Chr 7:12

REFLECTION. Our Lady of Guadalupe is still the great sign of the nearness of Christ with Whom she invites every human being to enter into communion.

She also invites all people into communion with one another in respect for each one's rights and in a just common sharing of the goods of this earth. —*Pope John Paul II*

PRAYER. *Most Blessed Virgin, Mother of the Poor, teach me to fight for justice for those who are oppressed. Help me to identify with the humble ones of this world, as you did when you appeared to Juan Diego.*

ET love be without pretense. Hate what is evil and hold to what is good. Love one another with mutual charity.
—Rom 12:9-10

REFLECTION. Love is great and authentic not only when it seems easy and pleasant, but also and most of all when it is strengthened in life's small and big trials. —*Pope John Paul II*

PRAYER. *O Lord, as Christmas draws near, there are so many things to do and I lose patience so easily. Let me not allow the trials of these days to rob my peace. Help me to see them as opportunities for greater efforts to be charitable.*

HOEVER drink of the water that I will give them will never thirst. The water ... will become in them a fountain of water, springing up to eternal life. —Jn 4:13-14

REFLECTION. Open your hearts to Christ and go out to meet Him; quench your thirst at His spring.

He offers a water that will satisfy your thirst for truth, for joy, for happiness, and for love. —*Pope John Paul II*

PRAYER. *Lord Jesus, let me drink deeply at the fountain of Your love. Let me sate my thirst with Your water of life, so that it may become in me a fountain of eternal life.*

 VERYONE who is angry with a brother or sister will be liable to judgment, and everyone who insults a brother or sister will be liable to the council. —Mt 5:22

REFLECTION. The peace of Christ can establish itself only where people are prepared to rid themselves of sin.

Those who do not live in peace with God can hardly live in peace with each other.

—*Pope John Paul II*

PRAYER. *O Lord, let me not curse evil in the world but uproot evil from my own heart. May I refuse to participate in evil and violence that so plagues our world even in the smallest way in which I might manipulate others.*

A ND the Word was made flesh and dwelt among us. And we saw His glory ... full of grace and truth.

DEC.
16

—Jn 1:14

REFLECTION. O Eternal Word of the Father, Son of God and of Mary, renew in our hearts the miracle of Your birth.

Clothe again with immortality the children You have redeemed, enkindle our love, bind all in Your Mystical Body. —*Pope John XXIII*

PRAYER. *Lord Jesus, as I prepare for the celebration of Your birth at Bethlehem, let me redouble my Advent commitment to prayer and conversion. Make my heart a welcome place for You to dwell in.*

N OW You dismiss Your servant O Lord, according to Your word in peace; because my eyes have seen Your salvation.

DEC.
17

—Lk 2:29-30

REFLECTION. How beautiful it is to open our spirit to the history of human life starting from the humble crib at Bethlehem.

Oh, the greatness of Christ's littleness! Oh, the coming of Christ at the human level of our lowliness in order to raise us to the heights of His divinity! —*Pope Paul VI*

PRAYER. *Lord Jesus, Your birth in Bethlehem puts in perspective our attempts to be great. Let me be satisfied with being little, humble, broken; for when I recognize my need, I create room for You.*

MAY God grant you to be strengthened with power through His Spirit ... and to have Christ dwelling in you through faith. —Eph 3:16-17

DEC. 18

REFLECTION. Let our God-Man return among us, our Lord acknowledged and obeyed, as at every Christmas time.

Christ returns in spirit to the crib and offers Himself to all. —Pope Pius XII

PRAYER. *Lord Jesus, be born again in my heart. May I say "Yes" to Your word in order to make You incarnate in this world again.*

GIVE, and it will be given to you; good measure, pressed down, shaken together, running over, will they pour into your lap. —Lk 6:38

DEC. 19

REFLECTION. No one can really enjoy Christmas without sharing that joy with those who, on this blessed day, still need food, work, a home, medical care, a friend, comfort, or faith.

The religious spirit of Christmas must find its expression in generosity. —Pope Paul VI

PRAYER. *O Lord, teach me that my Christmas preparations are not complete until I have developed a strategy for reaching out to the poor. Let me be like the shepherds who brought a lamb to the poor Child of Bethlehem.*

I AM the living Bread come down from heaven. Whoever eats of this Bread will live forever.

DEC. 20

—Jn 6:51-52

REFLECTION. Faith and life. These are nothing less than the realities in which we are immersed, and they are the goals to which we would draw attention.

Keep them particularly in mind during the coming happy occasion.

—Pope Paul VI

PRAYER. *O Lord, the celebration of Christmas draws near. Help me to view this feast in the perspective of my faith, in view of its promise of true life.*

 J OSEPH went from Nazareth into Judea ... to register together with Mary his espoused wife, who was with child.

DEC. 21

—Lk 2:4-5

REFLECTION. Do not be afraid to commit your life for others. Do not shy away from problems. Do not try to compromise with mediocrity or conformity.

It is time to assume your responsibilities, to become involved, not to run away.

—Pope John Paul II

PRAYER. *Father, it was difficult for Joseph and Mary to travel to Bethlehem. It demanded great trust in You. May I place my trust in You with equal courage.*

MEN, amen, I say to you, unless you be born again you cannot see the Kingdom of God.

—Jn 3:3

REFLECTION. With the coming of the birthday of the Redeemer, the Church would bring us to the stable of Bethlehem and there teach that we must be born again and undergo a complete reformation.

That will only happen when we are intimately and vitally united to the Word of God made Man. —*Pope Pius XII*

PRAYER. *O Lord, the great day draws ever nearer. Let Your love take root in my heart.*

———

HEY name Him ... Prince of Peace. There will be no end of the increase of His government and peace.

—Is 9:6-7

REFLECTION. All of us must be believers in peace, for ourselves and for the world, the peace that begins in our own hearts when we renounce hatred and evil and seek to overcome evil with good.

When it comes to peace we must be true believers; we must not lose hope in the message of Christmas. —*Pope John Paul II*

PRAYER. *O Lord, help me to contact one person during this Christmas season with whom I have not been getting along. May the birth of Jesus, Your Son, bring peace between us.*

WHEN the fullness of time arrived, God sent His Son, born of a woman,...that He might redeem those under the Law. —Gal 4:4-5

REFLECTION. Tomorrow, no tonight, we shall contemplate Him, meek and mild, a child like any other "born of woman." We shall be invited to admire and recognize Him, just as the shepherds once did.

He will bestow "grace and peace" on "all God's beloved who are called to be Saints."

—*Pope John Paul II*

PRAYER. *O come let us adore Him; O come let us adore Him; O come let us adore Him: Christ, the Lord.*

 MARY'S days to be delivered were fulfilled, and she brought forth her firstborn Son.

—Lk 2:6-7

REFLECTION. Look upon the Baby born in Bethlehem Who is beside His Mother Mary.

Draw near to Him, prostrate yourselves to adore Him, and offer Him the gifts that you bear in your heart.

—*Pope John Paul II*

PRAYER. *O Word of God, born as a child in Bethlehem. O God-Man, Creator Who have become creature. O Love incarnate. We all adore You. Come into my heart this day and teach me the real meaning of Christmas.*

HE wolf and the lamb will feed together.... They will neither harm nor destroy on My holy mountain.

DEC. 26

—Is 65:25

REFLECTION. O sweet and gentle Infant of Bethlehem, grant us the gift of sharing with our whole soul in this profound mystery of Christmas.

Put into other's hearts the peace that at times they seek so openly and that You alone can give them. —*Pope John XXIII*

PRAYER. *O Lord, let the wolf lie down with the lamb, the child play safely with the asp. Grant that there may be no harm anywhere on Your holy mountain.*

―――――――

 REATER love than this no one has, than to lay down one's life for one's friends.

DEC. 27

—Jn 15:13

REFLECTION. The measure of our love cannot be found simply in the weak capacity of the human heart. We must love according to the measure of the Heart of Christ.

With renewed conviction, proclaim your fidelity to Christ, the Redeemer of humanity.

—*Pope John Paul II*

PRAYER. *O Lord, so often I find that my love falls short and I cannot bring myself to forgive those who have hurt me or the ones I love. Fill my heart with Your forgiving love.*

A VOICE was heard in Rama, weeping and loud lamentation; Rachel weeping for her children, and she would not be comforted. —Mt 2:18

REFLECTION.   Human life is sacred. From its inception it reveals the creating hand of God.

Those who violate His laws offend the Divine Majesty and degrade themselves and humanity. They also sap the vitality of the political community of which they are members.

—*Pope John XXIII*

PRAYER. *O Lord, today we commemorate the sacrifice of the Holy Innocents. But the innocents are still dying; may I fight with all my might and resources to protect them.*

 WE have heard of your faith in Christ Jesus and of the love you bear toward all the holy ones. —Col 1:4

REFLECTION. Would it not be beautiful if Christmas were to generate the inner Christ within us: a habit of meditation, a living memory of the great Mystery that we have solemnly commemorated; a persuasion of faith, now acquired and confirmed?

We must live our lives in union with Christ's life.   —*Pope Paul VI*

PRAYER. *O Lord, may this Christmas season not end without my making a commitment to further growth in my spiritual life. Let this be my most precious Christmas present.*

HE wrapped Him in swaddling clothes and laid Him in a manger, because there was no room for them in the inn.

DEC. 30

—Lk 2:7

REFLECTION. No human riches could offer a fitting setting for the human birth of the eternal Son of God.

Only that poverty, that abandonment, that crib, that night at Bethlehem could provide it. It was fitting that He would not find lodging in that town. —*Pope John Paul II*

PRAYER. *Lord Jesus, You sought no comfort; You only sought to demonstrate Your love and identify with the poor. May I be a true disciple and follow Your example.*

N an acceptable time I have heard you. Behold, now is the acceptable time; behold, now is the day of salvation!

DEC. 31

—2 Cor 6:2

REFLECTION. Time is precious, it passes quickly. Time is a phase during which we make choices for our decisive and definitive state.

Our fidelity to our duties decides our future and eternal fate. Time is a gift from God.

—*Pope Paul VI*

PRAYER. *Lord, as this year draws to a close, teach me how precious time is. Let me never put off till tomorrow those words of love and forgiveness that I need to say today.*

HOLY WEEK

PALM SUNDAY

ND the crowds that went before Him, and those that followed, kept crying out, "Hosanna to the Son of David."

—Mt 21:9

REFLECTION. We are here to profess with victorious vigor that in Christ is the Way, the Truth, and the Life.

The explosion of our faith is so strong today that—as Jesus Himself said—if our voice were to keep silence, even the stones would cry out instead. —Pope Paul VI

PRAYER. *Lord Jesus, the crowd cried out "Hosanna," which means, "Lord, save us." I also cry out today with my voice and my heart, "Hosanna, Son of David."*

HOLY THURSDAY

ESUS took bread, and blessed and broke, and gave it to His disciples, and said, "Take and eat; this is My Body."

—Mt 26:26

REFLECTION. With the institution of the Eucharist, we enter into the very heart of humanity's drama.

Will it be life directed toward death, or life open to eternity! —Pope John Paul II

PRAYER. *Lord Jesus, the Eucharist is a re-presentation of Your sacrifice on the Cross. May I die with You to live with You forever.*

GOOD FRIDAY

 UT Jesus cried out with a loud voice and expired. And the curtain of the Temple was torn in two.

—Mk 15:37-38

REFLECTION. The journey also brings sacrifices, but these must not stop us.

Jesus is on the Cross: you want to kiss Him? You cannot help bending over the Cross and letting yourself be pricked by some thorns of the crown that is on the Lord's head.

—Pope John Paul I

PRAYER. *Lord, teach me not to run away from my cross or Your Cross, for by this Holy Cross You have redeemed the world.*

HOLY SATURDAY

 ECAUSE of the Preparation Day of the Jews, they laid Jesus in a new tomb in which no one had yet been laid.

—Jn 19:41-42

REFLECTION. The readings in the Paschal Vigil carry us into the mysterious arena where human sin meets God's justice and mercy.

There life and death "have contended," and there the victory of the risen Christ over death stands out as the source of our salvation and the model of Christian living.   —Pope Paul VI

PRAYER. *This day is filled with silence, Lord, as we await the outpouring of joy with which we will celebrate Your Resurrection. Help me to prepare diligently for that great event.*

EASTER SUNDAY

JESUS our Lord ... was handed over to death for our sins and was raised for our justification.

—Rom 4:24-25

REFLECTION. How can we not sing? How can we not express the fullness of those feelings accumulated during our long Lenten journey and during the dramatic ritual of the Paschal Triduum? —*Pope Paul VI*

PRAYER. *Alleluia. Death and sin have been conquered, life and love rule victorious. Alleluia.*

PRAYER FOR THE POPE

Lord Jesus Christ,
You willed to build Your Church on Peter the Rock
and the Popes who have succeeded him through the ages.
Pour forth Your grace on our Holy Father
that he may be a living sign and an indefatigable promoter
of the unity of the Church.
Help him to proclaim Your message to all people
and to listen to the message that comes to him
from the consensus of all its members
and from the world that You made.
Make him serve others after Your example
and in accord with his traditional title:
"Servant of the servants of God."
Unite us closely to him
and make us docile to his teachings.

OTHER OUTSTANDING BOOKS IN THIS SERIES

WORDS OF COMFORT FOR EVERY DAY—Short meditation for every day including a Scripture text and a meditative prayer to God the Father. Printed in two colors. 192 pages. **Ask for No. 186**

LEAD, KINDLY LIGHT—By Rev. James Sharp. Minute meditations for every day of the year taken from the writings of Cardinal Newman plus a concluding prayer for each day. **Ask for No. 184**

EVERY DAY IS A GIFT—Introduction by Most Rev. Frederick Schroeder. Popular meditations for every day, featuring a text from Sacred Scripture, a quotation from the writings of a Saint, and a meaningful prayer. **Ask for No. 195**

LARGE TYPE EDITION—This popular book offered in large, easy-to-read print. **Ask for No. 196**

MARY DAY BY DAY—Minute meditations for every day of the year, including a Scripture passage, a quotation from the Saints, and a concluding prayer. Printed in two colors with over 300 illustrations. **Ask for No. 180**

AUGUSTINE DAY BY DAY—By Rev. John Rotelle, O.S.A. Minute meditations for every day of the year taken from the writings of Augustine, with a concluding prayer also from the Saints. **Ask for No. 170**

BIBLE DAY BY DAY—By Rev. John Kersten, S.V.D. Minute Bible meditations for every day including a short Scripture text and brief reflection. Printed in two colors with 300 illustrations. **Ask for No. 150**

LIVING WISDOM FOR EVERY DAY—By Rev. Bennet Kelley, C.P. Choice texts from St. Paul of the Cross, one of the true Masters of Spirituality, and a prayer for each day. **Ask for No. 182**

MINUTE MEDITATIONS FOR EACH DAY— By Rev. Bede Naegele O.C.D. This very attractive book offers a short Scripture text, a practical reflection, and a meaningful prayer for each day of the year. **Ask for No. 190**

WHEREVER CATHOLIC BOOKS ARE SOLD

ISBN 978-0-89942-175-9

90000